TOGETHER AGAIN!

ALSO BY
GARSON KANIN

PLAYS
Born Yesterday   The Smile of the World
The Rat Race   The Live Wire
Come on Strong

Adaptations
The Amazing Adele   The Good Soup
A Gift of Time   Dreyfus in Rehearsal

NOVELS
Blow Up a Storm   A Thousand Summers
The Rat Race   One Hell of an Actor
Do Re Mi   Moviola
Where It's At   Smash

SHORT FICTION
Cast of Characters

FILMS
With Ruth Gordon
A Double Life   Adam's Rib
Pat and Mike   The Marrying Kind

In Collaboration
From This Day Forward   The More the Merrier
The True Glory

Original Stories
High Time   The Right Approach
The Girl Can't Help It

Original Screenplays
It Should Happen to You   Where It's At
Some Kind of a Nut

NONFICTION
Remembering Mr. Maugham   Felix Frankfurter: A Tribute
Tracy and Hepburn   Hollywood
It Takes a Long Time to Become Young

FILMS DIRECTED
A Man to Remember   My Favorite Wife
Next Time I Marry   They Knew What They Wanted
The Great Man Votes   Tom, Dick, and Harry
Bachelor Mother   Some Kind of a Nut
Where It's At

DOCUMENTARY FILMS
Ring of Steel   Battle Stations
(Spencer Tracy)   *(James Cagney/Ginger Rogers)*
Fellow Americans   Salute to France
(James Stewart)   *(Burgess Meredith/Claude Dauphin)*
The True Glory
(with Carol Reed)

PLAYS DIRECTED
Hitch Your Wagon   A Hole in the Head
Too Many Heroes   Small War on Murray Hill
The Rugged Path   The Good Soup
Born Yesterday   Sunday in New York
Years Ago   A Gift of Time
How I Wonder   Come on Strong
The Leading Lady   I Was Dancing
The Smile of the World   A Very Rich Woman
A Month in the Country   Remembering Mr. Maugham
The Rat Race   We Have Always Lived in the Castle
The Live Wire   Idiot's Delight *(revival)*
The Amazing Adele   Dreyfus in Rehearsal
Into Thin Air   Ho! Ho! Ho!
The Diary of Anne Frank

MUSICALS DIRECTED
Do Re Mi   Funny Girl
Fledermaus
(Metropolitan Opera Company)

TOGETHER AGAIN!

The Stories of the Great Hollywood Teams

by

GARSON KANIN

Designed by William McCaffery

Doubleday & Company, Inc.
Garden City, New York

My grateful thanks to my friend and associate,
JEAN H. LENAUER, for his indefatigable and
creative research, which made the making
of this book such a joy.

And to BETH CURTIN,
without whom...

And to Manuel Rosario.

And to Samuel S. Vaughan,
for endless unflagging enthusiasm.

Grateful acknowledgment is made to the photograph
collection of the Museum of Modern Art Film Stills
Archives and Movie Star News for their cooperation.

Grateful acknowledgment is also made to the following
motion picture studios: Metro-Goldwyn-Mayer, Warner Brothers,
Paramount Pictures, RKO Pathé, Universal Pictures, United Artists,
Cinema V, Columbia Pictures, Hal Roach, Embassy Pictures, Fox,
Twentieth Century–Fox.

CONTENTS

INTRODUCTION

Life, as a rule, is created by a TEAM in passionate action.

Two heads are better than one, and so are two bodies, two pairs of arms, two sets of hands, in short—two of everything.

Men and women reach the apex of existence when coupled.

We all understand and appreciate the TEAM idea in sports: baseball, basketball, football. The dependence and interdependence of individuals makes for power.

The idealization of the TEAM concept has been represented on film since the earliest days of the Silver Screen.

Think of them. Remember the special joys that were found in these matings: Fred Astaire and Ginger Rogers, Spencer Tracy and Katharine Hepburn, William Powell and Myrna Loy—(notice how often the man's name came first?)—Jeanette MacDonald and Nelson Eddy—(well, not *always*)—Mickey Rooney and Judy Garland, Douglas Fairbanks and Mary Pickford, Greta Garbo and John Gilbert, Laurence Olivier and Vivien Leigh. The list goes on and on, as we will observe.

In mathematics, one plus one indubitably equals two. $1 + 1 = 2$. In movies, one plus one may well equal one hundred and one. $1 + 1 = 101$.

The question is: What makes a great TEAM? The words and pictures that lie ahead do not supply the answer—but they do examine the question in depth, and to the extent that you, the reader, will probably be able to supply your own answers.

Unless one believes that marriages are made in Heaven, the making of TEAMS is equally mysterious.

In Hollywood, it is sometimes referred to as the He-She Chemistry. Spencer Tracy and Lana Turner. Nothing. Spencer Tracy and Hedy Lamarr. No. Spencer Tracy and Jean Harlow. Better. Spencer Tracy and Deborah Kerr. Pale. Spencer Tracy and Katharine Hepburn. Bingo! Jackpot! A TEAM.

Two men may similarly possess what is called Chemistry. Paul Newman and Robert Redford. Victor McLaglen and Edmund Lowe.

Bob Hope and Bing Crosby (or was that a ménage à trois with Dorothy Lamour?). Or three men: The Three Stooges. Or four men: The Marx Brothers. Or two women: Marie Dressler and Polly Moran.

A magical matching takes place, and we are given living proof that once in a wonderful while—life rhymes.

Some TEAMS were created for commercial purposes—others were born completely by accident.

Examples: When MGM decided to film Dashiell Hammett's American classic, THE THIN MAN, they did so because William Powell, who was under contract to them, had had great success playing the detective Philo Vance. Powell as a detective, then, appeared to be what the audience wanted, and MGM was devoted to the idea of giving the audience what it wanted.

Now, in addition to Nick Charles, Hammett had created Nora Charles, his wife. Who to play it? MGM had under contract at the time thirteen Big Star women, twenty-two minor leading ladies, and twenty-nine supporting actresses. Myrna Loy was in the second category. She specialized in exotic characters, sloe-eyed temptresses, denizens of the inscrutable East. (A line for which she was well-known: "De geepsies dey tich me to walk so as nevair to crosh a flowaire.") How, then, did she achieve Nora? It turned out that of the thirteen Biggies, six were unavailable, two refused to appear in what might be termed a "B" picture or at most a "nervous A." Three others thought the role of Nora unequal to that of Nick. The remaining two claimed to be ill. And so on to the next list. Interviews were conducted, tests were made.

"How about Loy?" asked an assistant casting director, putting his job in jeopardy.

But W. S. Van Dyke, the maverick director, thought it worth a try. Powell, who admired Myrna Loy's acting, offered to test with her. The result was electrifying. A TEAM was born, Jovelike, and was to create a style, a world, an untold amount of joy, and millions for MGM.

A manufactured TEAM, a lucky shot.

Conversely, there is the story of Astaire and Rogers.

Ginger Rogers was a minor contract player at RKO. A producer named Lou Brock was making a musical called FLYING DOWN TO RIO, starring Gene Raymond and Dolores Del Rio. Vincent Youmans had come up with a song, "The Carioca," which clearly called for a dance number:

"Oh, have you seen the Carioca?
It's not a fox trot or a polka . . ."

Ginger, who had danced successfully on Broadway (GIRL CRAZY) and on the screen (GOLD DIGGERS OF 1933) was called upon. Came the question of a partner. A Latin was sought but not immediately found.

As it happened, MGM had that same month brought Fred Astaire from New York (his sister and teammate, Adele, had married Lord Cavendish and left the stage) to do a number in DANCING LADY with Joan Crawford (a former .Charleston champion). The dance had gone well enough, but the front office was dismayed by Fred Astaire's looks. "Too small" read a memo to the East. "Also bald, big ears, skinny, jutting jaw—impossible to photograph."

So there was no question of his continuing at MGM. The Crawford number was tantamount to a screen test, and he had failed it miserably.

It is difficult to say for certain now who it was who suggested that RKO take Astaire off MGM's hands—it might indeed have been MGM, although no one there has ever admitted it. At RKO, however, everyone connected with FLYING DOWN TO RIO has claimed the credit.

Does it matter?

The fact is that Astaire came to RKO, did "The Carioca" with Ginger Rogers, and changed the size and shape and personality of the American screen musical for all time.

Astaire and Rogers made ten lovely films together, employing the scores of Cole Porter, George and Ira Gershwin, Jerome Kern and Dorothy Fields, Irving Berlin, and others.

A world to remember fondly, and, fortunately, preserved for all time.

What then is the essence of a TEAM?

In Astaire and Rogers, contrast. He, the smooth, sophisticated, urbane, and elegant man of the world; she, the game, open, lively, sexy girl of the people. They meet, they have an effect upon each other. They find a common plateau—in the clouds—and share it. They sing. They dance. They love. The End.

Contrast. Of course.

But where is the contrast in the Powell-Loy TEAM?

Both elegant and sophisticated. Moreover —where's the suspense in their screen relationship? They're *married*, for God's sake. They always *have* been married, they always *will* be.

A puzzle.

Some romantic TEAMS were so on screen and off. Humphrey Bogart and Lauren Bacall (married). Greta Garbo and John Gilbert (un).

Astaire and Rogers, on the other hand, had little contact off screen.

So TEAMS are charming, mysterious—as curious as those we know in the lives about us.

"What does he see in her?"

"What does she see in him?"

"What a charming couple!"

One thing, however, seems clear to one who has pondered the question in the dark for years—all TEAMS of two are Male and Female. Boldly male and coyly female. Passively female and actively male. Powerfully male and tenderly female. Coquettish female and desiring male. Definitely He and oh boy She.

Even in the man-and-man TEAMS, the division holds. Paul Newman and Robert Redford. Which is which?

Marie Dressler and Polly Moran. Who is who?

Finally, consider that even in some of our celebrated He-She Chemistries—the female is sometimes the He and the male the She. Just like in real life—if there is a real life.

A Woman of Affairs   *1929*

The Silent Lovers
GRETA GARBO and JOHN GILBERT

Imagine that you are a shopper in the massive P.U.B. department store in Stockholm in the early 1920's. It is entirely possible that the buxom young salesgirl waiting on you is Greta Louisa Gustafsson. Would you have noticed anything special about her? Probably not. Who could have conceived that she would in a short time become the most beautiful, glamorous, mysterious, desirable woman of the twentieth century?

The enterprising public-relations man for the store decided to make a short film clip to be used as advertising in motion-picture theatres.

The public-relations man wandered about the store, casting. Using one of the salesgirls would save money. He selected four and had them come up to his office after hours to model clothing, smile, demonstrate cosmetics. He chose Miss Gustafsson. The clip was shot and shown. A success. Two more film clips were made. She was paid $3.00 a day for making these films. She felt, she recalls, like a movie star.

If you should ever find yourself in Stockholm, go to the Filmhistorical Archives and ask to see the print of Greta Garbo's debut film. What will surprise you is to see that it is actually a comedy, not precisely what made Greta

Garbo's American career. The film you will see has to do with teaching ladies to dress beautifully. Miss Gustafsson's part is the comedy relief; she demonstrates how *not* to dress. She comes in clumsily, wearing an oversized dress with a checkered skirt and checkered scarf. She models the horror happily and then does a trick transformation, turning her costume into a riding habit.

This picture was directed by Captain Ragnar Ring, who was in the business of producing commercial films.

Her success in the fashion film led to another job, this one for the specialties of the Consumers Cooperative Association of Stockholm. She did little in it but eat French pastry.

Then in 1922, Erik Petschler, a minor Swedish film director, came in to the P.U.B. to outfit two of his leading ladies. Miss Gustafsson waited on them. Needless to say, she was by this time hopelessly screen-struck. She asked Petschler for advice on the process of getting into films. He auditioned her and offered her a job in the picture he was about to start. Miss Gustafsson tried to change her vacation schedule so that she could accept his offer without losing her steady job.

The Archives has her employment card. On one dotted line of the form are the words: "Reason for Leaving." Opposite this is written: "To enter the films."

And that is precisely what she did. She took the great gamble, gave up her job, and embarked on the treacherous journey.

It should be borne in mind that she had no training whatsoever. The department store was hardly an academy of dramatic art. Before that, her job was a *tvalflicka*, which required her to lather men's faces in Einer Wideback's barbershop, was not equivalent to a provincial repertory theatre.

Her first picture was called LUFFAR-PETTER (PETER THE TRAMP).

It convinced Miss Gustafsson that she needed some training. She contacted Petschler and asked him about getting into the Royal Dramatic Theatre Academy. He arranged for her to be coached for her audition by the daughter of a former Academy director. Miss Gustafsson was then sixteen years old. She was coached in a scene from DUNUNGEN by Selma Lagerlöf. Also in a scene from MADAME SANS-GENE by Sardou. And finally, a short scene from THE LADY FROM THE SEA by Ibsen.

At the audition, she did her first two scenes and was dismissed. She was sure this meant rejection, but three or four days later, she was informed by letter that she had been accepted. So in September 1922 she entered the Royal Dramatic Theatre Academy.

Before the end of the first term, the director of the Academy, Gustaf Molander, sent for her and for a second-year student named Mona Martenson. He explained to the two girls that Mauritz Stiller had asked him to recommend two girls to be tested. Mauritz Stiller, a Russian Jewish émigré, was at that time the most important movie director in Sweden. The next morning, the Misses Gustafsson and Martenson reported to the studios at Svensk Filmindustri.

There are men who have a filmic eye, and Mauritz Stiller was one of them. Others looked at Miss Gustafsson and saw an overweight, ungainly, inexperienced, naive, peasantlike beginner. Stiller looked at her, long and hard, and saw Greta Garbo. He explained that he wanted her to change her name because Gustafsson was too Swedish. He wanted something international in flavor. He asked the head of his story department for suggestions. The one that came back was "Mona Gabor." Stiller thought highly of the "Mona" but felt that "Gabor" was too Hungarian. He began to twist the letters about, looking for a more international quality, and hit upon "Garbo." Mona Garbo. Say it. Mona Garbo. Say it again. It was decided. Mona Garbo it would be. Miss Gustafsson said she understood about changing her surname, but refused to give up Greta. After some struggle, "Greta Garbo" was considered. Say it. Greta Garbo. Say it again. Greta Garbo. Greta Garbo it was.

How curious that the part of the name she clung to, Greta, was largely abandoned by the world that came to adore her, and bestowed upon her the most distinguished of accolades, referring to her simply as "Garbo."

Stiller put her into the leading role of his picture, GOSTA BERLING'S SAGA.

A strange arrangement was worked out. She was to continue her studies at the Academy while making the picture. On the days when she was not required on the set, she attended classes.

The picture was no more than a mild success in Sweden, but a smash hit in Berlin, and Greta Garbo was well and truly launched.

As a result of this, she got a job with G. W. Pabst, playing the lead in the film called THE STREET OF SORROW. It was not a success, yet did a great deal to advance her career.

L. B. Mayer, visiting Berlin, saw a screening of GOSTA BERLING'S SAGA. He was not terribly impressed with the leading lady, but thought the picture and its direction superlative. Mayer sent for Mauritz Stiller and offered him a contract. Stiller said he would accept on one condition: that Mayer also sign Greta Garbo.

So it was arranged. Svengali Stiller and Trilby Garbo were off to Hollywood, where he was to suffer humiliation and finally defeat, while she was to achieve the position of the greatest screen personality of her time, mainly because she created black-and-white shadows that were far more affecting and telling than actual flesh and blood.

Kenneth Tynan said it best: "What, when drunk, one sees in other women, one sees in Garbo sober."

Part of the tragedy of this incomparable but largely wasted artist lies in the fact that her beauty and celebrity and notoriety conspired to obscure a truly great acting talent. As proof, one has only to recall the luminous magic of Garbo in THE TEMPTRESS, ANNA CHRISTIE, CAMILLE, NINOTCHKA, ANNA KARENINA, GRAND HOTEL, QUEEN CHRISTINA, AS YOU DESIRE ME, MATA HARI, ROMANCE—among the twenty-seven films she made before her retirement in 1942, at the age of thirty-six.

Metro-Goldwyn-Mayer was the only studio by which she was ever employed in America. The executives there, following the death of Irving Thalberg, may have known how to deal with starlets, comics, sexpots, dancers, singers, child stars, and the like, but they were flummoxed in the face of genius.

The cruel and shattering treatment she suffered at their hands may have been sufficiently traumatic to immobilize her artistically following her final picture, TWO-FACED WOMAN.

How this mindless trifle ever reached the screen remains an irritating mystery. Think of it: Larry Blake (Melvyn Douglas) meets and marries Karin, a skiing instructress (Greta Garbo), while on a holiday. When he returns to New York, he is again attracted by his ex-wife, Griselda Vaughn (Constance Bennett). Shall we stop right here for a moment? "Look, fellas, Connie is swell and all that—but are we going to ask an audience to believe that Mel, having wooed and what's more, *won* Garbo—is going to dump her—walk out on her—reject her? Garbo? For Connie Bennett?" The unfortunate questioner is off the picture. Back to the story. There is worse to come.

Garbo, abandoned by Melvyn Douglas, naturally wants to get him back. Of course. But how? How would *you* go about getting him back? How would anyone? Have no fear. The inventive faculties of highly paid screenwriters always come through in a pinch. "Fellas, there's only *one way* that hasn't been done, and it'll work. To get him back, see, Garbo poses as her own twin sister, see? It'll work. Didn't it work in *The Guardsman?* She poses as her *own twin sister!* Maybe with a dark wig or something, or maybe not—whatever. Anyway, she's her own twin sister, and the audience knows it, but he doesn't, and she comes on and makes it. You know, seduces him and gets him back. Then she naturally tells him and maybe he claims he knew it all the time, or maybe not—whatever. But anyway, the main thing is she gets him back! Terrific?"

Good God! How could this have been perpetrated? It is difficult enough to believe in the existence of *one* Garbo—and here we are asked to believe there are *two*.

To compound the insult, this schnitzel followed the utterly delightful NINOTCHKA, written by Charles Brackett and Billy Wilder, and directed by the incomparable Ernst Lubitsch.

About two weeks after shooting began, a furious L. B. Mayer stopped production.

"She looks the same when she's the sister as when she's not!" he screamed. L. B., it should be remembered, was a man who lived at the top of his voice.

"But, Mr. Mayer—she's supposed to be the *twin* sister!"

Another man off the picture.

Hairdressers are summoned. Makeup men are called in. Designers bullied. Working together, they succeed in pacifying L. B. Mayer and ruining one-half of Garbo's performance.

Here is the great Ernst Lubitsch on the subject of Greta Garbo:

"She is a very unusual girl. She gets quite worried about scenes. She had to play a drunk scene, for instance, in *Ninotchka* and do the scene in a public restaurant, but I realized soon that she was full of inhibitions and disliked playing the scene in front of all the extras. So she came to me and said, 'I don't think that I can play it.' That was my signal for action. 'Look here,' I said. 'I'll do anything you want. I'll change the script, the dialogue, but this can't be changed. Too much depends on it. You must make up your mind that you'll have to play it.' After that, of course, she had to continue. . . . When you see it in the picture, you'll find that she plays it delightfully. So real. Not the routine of an actor who uses the customary tools. That's why it's charming. . . . It is not at all difficult to work with Garbo. To be sure, there is the fact that she breaks at five o'clock and nothing can make her work after that hour. Even if the scene is not done, it has to be postponed until the next day. This might sound at the very moment very annoying to a director, as if she were arbitrary. Yet, on the other hand, she is ready to shoot, dressed and made up, at nine o'clock in the morning. She feels that working from nine to five is all she can stand physically.

"Having worked with many women stars, I have found that one of the difficulties with them is their slavish devotion to the mirror. Some of them take a terribly long time to powder and make up between scenes. They are so much concerned about their looks that they exhaust their vitality. In the eight weeks during which I worked with Greta Garbo, she never looked into the mirror once unless I told her to do so. Nobody but the moving picture director can appreciate the significance of this fact.

"Garbo never looks at rushes. She feels that in doing so, she might be so depressed that she couldn't go on. Therefore, she relies entirely on what the director tells her the next morning. The first time she saw her work in *Ninotchka* was the first preview after the picture was cut and edited. When I asked her, 'Do you like yourself in it?' even then she didn't seem to know if she was bad or good."

John Gilbert was quite another story. A child of the Pringles, a pair of third-rate stock players, he was theatrical from birth. He went on the stage before he began to record memories, thus he remembered no time when he was not a professional player.

At sixteen, he determined to try his luck in California. Although he was already remarkably handsome, he was too young to play leading parts. In fact, he found that there were few parts for which he was suitable. So he went to work at the Ince Studio as a stagehand, handyman, extra, man of all work.

The tragic elements of his life began early. While working at Ince, he fell in love with a beautiful little extra named Effie. One day during shooting, an enormous set collapsed. Effie was killed. Gilbert, grief-stricken, decided to leave California, to leave the movie business forever. In time, he was talked out of this rash act and returned to work.

Years went by, and although he was well liked and hardworking, progress was slow. He was assigned a few bits now and then, but no more. Handsome young men were not in short supply.

Stage stars from New York arrived at the Ince Studio with great regularity: Julia Dean, Frank Keenan, Billie Burke, Dorothy Dalton, William Collier, and finally a beautiful creature named Enid Bennett, who had made a great success playing opposite Otis Skinner in COCK O' THE WALK.

A picture was planned for her called PRINCESS OF THE DARK. Mr. Ince astonished Gilbert one morning with the news that he was being considered to play opposite Enid Bennett, and moreover, was going to be given a two-year contract. He would receive $30 a week the first year, and $40 a week the second year. What mattered to Gilbert more than anything was the fact that his new position made it unnecessary for him to punch the time clock.

The picture turned out to be a failure, but worse—he failed to make any particular impression.

PRINCESS OF THE DARK is one of the many lost pictures, but in this case the loss is minor. This was the story: Enid Bennett played the part of a little blind girl. John Gilbert played a crippled boy with a twisted leg and a hump on his back. Both of them acted as hard as they could, perhaps too hard. After the picture was shown, Gilbert's name was added to the roster of extras once again.

Another young player on the lot, Irwin Willat, a friend of Gilbert's, was made a director, and given a picture to do. Gilbert was unlucky enough to be standing within earshot of the new director when he heard his name suggested for a part.

Anna Christie *1931*

"My God, no," said Willat. "He's terrible. Besides, his nose looks Jewish."

Here, in Gilbert's own words, is his reaction:

"My heart turned cold. I hid myself in my dark dressing room—and struggled with this great tragic problem. My career as an actor was unquestionably over. No hope for me now. I gazed long into my mirror and burst into tears. The reflection in the glass before me became a loathsome thing. What madness had led me to believe myself capable of pleasing audiences with such a countenance? I sobbed bitterly, and not until darkness came did I attempt to show my face beyond my dressing room. Then I dragged my weary carcass away—a broken, pitiable remnant of what I had thought was a dynamic, forceful man."

Ridiculous as it may seem, this experience had a permanent effect upon Gilbert, a shock from which he was never to recover. He was unable to see himself through his own eyes, but for the rest of his life, saw himself through the eyes of Irwin Willat. He hated himself on the screen and bent every effort to leave acting and become a writer or a director or both. In fact, he did a great deal of writing for the screen.

His early attempts, however, were poor indeed, by his own admission, and he was forced to return to acting.

World War I came, and he wanted to enlist. He tried first for the Air Corps, but enlistments there were closed. He went to the Navy's recruiting offices and was rejected for lack of education.

He went back to work, scrounging about for bits until the draft came. He was classified as 1-A, but was not called up until November 11, 1918, the day the war ended.

In the meantime, he had blundered into his first marriage—there were to be many.

His career was going badly. "I must get out of acting as a means of livelihood. I knew that. Out of acting—out of acting! Too tall, too short, too fat, too thin, hair wrong color, eyes wrong color, nose too long, hands too—hell!! Would it never end?"

Distracted and discouraged, he left his young wife. "The Los Angeles Athletic Club lured me. There I could meet friends and contemporaries. The gymnasium and swimming

14

His Glorious Night   *1921*

pool would put on much-needed weight." (At 5 feet 11 inches, he weighed 115 pounds.) "One's residence there lent certain prestige to one's name.

"I moved to the club. The first night at dinner, at a great round table in the grill, I sat —awed, before the famous ones about me— Charlie Chaplin, Dick Barthelmess, Bobby Harron, Ray Griffith, Marshall Neilan, James Kirkwood, Tony Moreno—and more. They seemed so gay and rich and successfully happy. I hoped that I would one day attain their lack of self-consciousness. I never have."

Although he was known as John Gilbert on the screen, the profession knew him only as "Jack" Gilbert. He was engaged by the distinguished French director, Maurice Tourneur, as a leading man. During the course of the shooting, Tourneur quarreled with his assistant and fired him. Gilbert immediately asked for the job.

"But you are my leading man," said Tourneur.

"I'll be your assistant, too," said Jack.

What he had in mind was using this as a training ground to become a director himself.

Another associate of Tourneur was Clarence Brown, who was later to direct Garbo and Gilbert in FLESH AND THE DEVIL. Brown was having great difficulty getting a satisfactory script and talked over his problem informally one day with Gilbert, who immediately began to make suggestions. Brown, desperate, asked Gilbert to work on the script. In three days and three nights, Gilbert rewrote THE GREAT REDEEMER. Tourneur was delighted. He now had an assistant director, a scenario writer, and a leading man, all rolled into one.

Then Jack Gilbert met the beautiful Leatrice Joy, and the second of his marriages followed soon after.

Gilbert's career began to move with THE COUNT OF MONTE CRISTO, CAMEO KIRBY, THE MERRY WIDOW, and then his unforgettable performance in King Vidor's THE BIG PARADE.

At this point, he was considered to be the greatest male star in films.

Then came his films with Greta Garbo: FLESH AND THE DEVIL, LOVE—a version of ANNA KARENINA, A WOMAN OF AFFAIRS. This film was based upon Michael Arlen's play, THE GREEN

Flesh and the Devil   *1927*

A Woman of Affairs   *1929*

Queen Christina   *1933*

Flesh and the Devil   *1927*

Love *1927*

Love *1927*

Queen Christina *1933*

Flesh and the Devil *1927*

HAT. The title had to be changed to satisfy the Hays office, which had banned THE GREEN HAT as immoral. In its wondrous way, the Hays office approved the picture without change so long as it was released under a different title.

Shortly after their first film began shooting, the rumors of their love affair gained national attention.

There was a story that they were engaged. Another that they were already married. In time, the studio insisted they say something.

John Gilbert: "There was too much trouble over that question once before. Every newspaper in the country carried stories that we were about to be married. It wouldn't be fair to Miss Garbo for me to say anything at all."

Greta Garbo: "I have no control over what is said or printed, but I am not engaged to Mr. Gilbert and I am not going to be. John is a fine boy and I like him immensely, but there are going to be no wedding bells—or even diamonds."

The MGM publicity department made great news of the fact that in the fourth reel of LOVE, John Gilbert kisses Greta Garbo eighty-nine times.

And they were delighted when on June 11, 1928, the film was banned in Westwood, New Jersey.

At the premiere of the picture on December 20, 1927, the famous radio announcer, Ted Husing of WPAP, broadcast the first so-called telemovie and for ninety minutes without a stop, he relayed to his listeners every move made in the picture, describing it somewhat as he used to describe sporting events.

The fan magazines, as may be imagined, had themselves a time. One of them, *Screen Classic*, in its issue of November 1927 gushed as follows:

"You can't take John Gilbert's ardent nature away from him. The favorite of the flappers speaks a language understood by every fluttering heart. If you don't think he is pretty keen for Greta Garbo, then your eyes are in need of a pair of cheaters. And how Greta takes it is nobody's business. John and Greta have the folks standing in line for hours to see them do their stuff. And how they do it! Some of the boys study John's technique so as to practice it on their girlfriends. Between the two of them, they are making the world a more romantic place to live in. Their loving ways may be seen in LOVE."

During the making of A WOMAN OF AFFAIRS, Clarence Brown, the director, wanted to enlarge Gilbert's part. The Garbo-Gilbert romance was at its height. Clarence Brown reports:

"As you know, his part was somewhat subordinate to Miss Garbo's role, and when I offered to put a bit more business in for him, so that he'd have more footage, Jack kicked like a steer. He was afraid any tampering with the part—a weakling's part—might strengthen it too much and ruin our story. That's a case of pure idealism and unselfishness in an actor."

Their romance, highly publicized and mysterious, was short-lived.

Gilbert's career went downhill after the coming of sound, but Garbo made a stunning talkie debut in ANNA CHRISTIE and her success soared.

The affair was over, and so was the teaming, but when the powerful Garbo was cast in QUEEN CHRISTINA, she managed to get the studio to fire Laurence Olivier and replace him with John Gilbert.

Garbo's gesture, well-intentioned as it was, failed badly. Among the reviews for QUEEN CHRISTINA are these depressing excerpts:

"John Gilbert doesn't make his comeback. His role is too small and he is forced into the background and given little chance."

"John Gilbert makes a notable reappearance as her lover—though not quite that great lover of former days."

"For John Gilbert, this film is supposed to be the supreme test whether he is to renew his former screen prominence, but his part as a young ambassador is so entirely subordinated to that of the star that he does not get much chance of distinguishing himself. His performance is adequate, but he is hardly that great lover of former days."

By 1933, it was virtually over for Jack Gilbert. The sentimental and heartwarming gesture on the part of his former love had no lasting effect. He died three years later.

A Woman of Affairs *1929*

A Woman of Affairs *1929*

Queen Christina *1933*

Queen Christina *1933*

Queen Christina *1933*

Queen Christina *1933*

Anyone who can sit through a Garbo-Gilbert film without being warmly affected in the regions that matter is either asexual or dead.

All but one of their pictures is a silent, which somehow adds to the wonder.

Those pulsating images on the screen provide material for the stimulation of the imagination that is unbounded in its possibilities. Sexual congress on the highest plane needs no words—the act has a powerful language of its own.

Even in the stillness of these stills the sensations emanate. Two hungering lives are being drawn to one another magnetically, confident of gratification.

Their off-screen love affair was inevitable, particularly since neither of them was married at the time of their meeting. The steamy scenes they were called upon to perform must have been arousing in the extreme, and since union was impossible—or at least impractical—on the screen, the relationship moved into privacy.

Miss Garbo, a private person, found her real-life pairing with John Gilbert strange. For he, conversely, was a merry, gregarious, active rounder. Fun-loving Jack.

They shared much, however, and one of the things they had in common was their mutual loathing of interviews. They thought the practice a rude intrusion and could not see the benefits other than the justification of the studio's vast publicity department and the convenience of the proliferating fan magazines—sixty-six of them being simultaneously published in the United States.

At length Gilbert found a way to be relieved for good from the nuisance of being interviewed.

The studio had forced him into an on-the-set interview with Ruth Waterbury of *Photoplay* magazine. She was a prim and proper young lady, new to Hollywood.

She asked the usual questions and received the accustomed answers until she inquired, "And how did you happen to become an actor, Mister Gilbert?"

"Oh," he replied, "it was ordained. My mother and my father, you see, were both on

the stage. Yes. They ran the stock company in Salt Lake City, and I went on whenever they needed a child in the play."

"How fascinating," said Miss Waterbury.

"Yes, isn't it? I recall once taking a curtain call with my parents after the first act of a play —we took calls after each act in those days—my mother was wearing a long dress with a bustle and a train—it was a period piece. Well, she stepped forward to take her solo call—we had one of those roll-up curtains that rolled up and down like an enormous window shade—and somehow the train of my mother's gown got caught in the roll curtain, and up, up, up it went. And do you know," he said, his eyes misty with memory, "that was the last time I ever saw my mother's ass."

"Thank you," said the stunned-out-of-her-wits Miss Waterbury as she fled.

And do you know—that was the last time John Gilbert ever saw an interviewer's pad.

The Hollywood legend has it that the talkies ruined Gilbert's career, that his voice came out high and squeaky and effeminate, and that audiences could no longer accept him as a leading man or as a lover.

I accepted this story, even repeated it. Yet from time to time, there would be hints of darker doings. Why would John Gilbert have had a poor voice? It had never been remarked upon. He had, after all, had some success as a stage player. Could he have done so with a squeaky voice? The story of his downfall has had more than one set of apocryphal details.

Recently, his daughter by Leatrice Joy, Leatrice Gilbert Fountain, gave the following account:

"I grew up thinking of my father as a has-been movie star. I saw him out when he died— I was eleven at the time—and it's true that he had a problem with alcohol. But he took terrible punishment from L. B. Mayer, and he took it gracefully. For quite some time, they had a series of minor squabbles. My father was very close to Irving Thalberg, which irritated Mayer, and he hung out with literati, with Mencken and Carey Wilson and Herman Mankiewicz. Those men were my father's friends,

and they were Democrats and liberals. Mayer's daughter, Irene Selznick, told me that every time he had been out with John Gilbert, he came home quivering with rage.

"It would be difficult to prove that they tampered with the sound on my father's first talkie, but my mother, who was in vaudeville then, saw it in Milwaukee, and she said that his voice in the movie was nothing like his real voice. He had grown up in the theatre and he was a serious actor with a wonderful speaking voice. It wasn't even a tenor; it was a high baritone. Clarence Brown told me that he ran into Douglas Shearer, Norma's brother, who was head of the sound department at MGM, and he asked him what on earth had happened to Jack's voice. 'My God,' Shearer said, 'didn't you know? We made a mistake and forgot to turn up the bass. We only turned up the treble.' I've also heard it said that Lionel Barrymore, who directed *His Glorious Night,* was paid a lot of money by Mayer to scuttle the movie any way he could.

"Mayer and my father had tolerated one another until the day of September eighth, nineteen twenty-six. That was to be the day of a double wedding at Marion Davies's house in Beverly Hills. King Vidor was to marry Eleanor Boardman and my father was to marry Greta Garbo. Garbo did not show up, and Eleanor Boardman told me years later what took place. My father was very upset, and Mayer said to him, 'Why do you have to *marry* her? Why not just sleep with her and forget about her?' With that, my father slugged him and dragged him into the bathroom and began hitting his head against the tiles, sending his glasses flying. Eddie Mannix, Mayer's trusted friend and bodyguard, finally pulled Father off him. Like a cobra, Mayer sat there and hissed, 'Gilbert, your career is finished. I'll destroy you if it costs me a million dollars!' "

That sounds like L. B. Mayer, all right. A costly enemy—and the serpent in the garden of Greta Garbo and John Gilbert.

Anna Christie *1931*

Jeanette MacDonald and Maurice Chevalier

Jeanette MacDonald + Jack Buchanan

Jeanette MacDonald + DeNNis KING

Jeanette MacDonald and Gene Raymond

Jeanette MacDonald + Nelson Eddy

NELSON EDDY
+
ELEANOR POWELL

Nelson Eddy
and
Virginia Bruce

Nelson Eddy
and
Ilona Massey

Nelson Eddy
+
Jeanette
MacDonald

Nelson Eddy
+
Risë Stevens

Rose-Marie *1936*

Harmony, Inc.
JEANETTE MacDONALD and NELSON EDDY

Someone, long ago, asked Russel Crouse, "Do you like operettas?"

"Only telephone operettas," he replied.

A fine fast crack in a day when operettas were a staple of the entertainment world, and telephone operators (easy targets for dalliance) were a living part of everyday existence.

Ah, well. Dial and push-button equipment have all but replaced the charm of casual contact with the human voice. Who can relate flirtatiously to a machine? Hail and farewell, you darling telephone operettas!

And musical operettas have just about vanished, as well. Time was when the so-called Shubert operettas blanketed the country. Eight companies of BLOSSOM TIME, six of THE STUDENT PRINCE, four of MAYTIME, six of THE MERRY WIDOW, and who knows how many of THE VAGABOND KING.

The Shuberts were by no means the only champions of the form. Their competitors presented, among others, such shows as THE FIREFLY, THE THREE MUSKETEERS, THE DESERT SONG, THE CHOCOLATE SOLDIER, SWEETHEARTS, and NAUGHTY MARIETTA.

Millions of happy theatregoers paid hundreds of millions of dollars to see and hear these productions.

Thus, when sound came to the screen, it did not require giant brains to conceive the idea that operettas could succeed commercially.

As early as 1929, Ernst Lubitsch decided to make THE LOVE PARADE as his first talkie for Paramount. A musical, to star his favorite, Maurice Chevalier. The search for a leading lady began. Lubitsch was told that the eastern office had tested a number of promising actresses in the preceding year. He went to New York to see the tests, as well as the current shows.

None of the people in shows appealed to him, but one of the testees did. Who was she? Jeanette MacDonald, a girl from Philadelphia, who had begun as a dancer, developed into a singer, and was at this time a fairly well-known Broadway musical-comedy player.

Her test—a scene from NOTHING BUT THE TRUTH—had been made during the short New York run of a show called BOOM BOOM, in which she had played the lead. On the same day, another player in the company also had made a test. He was Archie Leach—later Cary Grant.

Neither MacDonald nor Leach had made it at that time.

"What kind of singer is she?" asked Lubitsch. "I have this beautiful score by Victor Schertzinger, and I must not crooners or deedle-dee-dee."

He was told that MacDonald was currently playing BOOM BOOM in Chicago. Being Lubitsch, he lost no time in getting there.

Two days later, he had his leading lady, and she had the beginning of a splendid film career.

THE LOVE PARADE, starring Maurice Chevalier and featuring Jeanette MacDonald, was a rousing success. She sang "Dream Lover" and "The March of the Grenadiers." He did "Nobody's Using It Now" and "My Love Parade." It was a film worthy of René Clair, who had doubtless influenced it.

Paramount, delighted with their new star, put her at once into THE VAGABOND KING by Rudolf Friml—and doubly insured the sure-fire hit by engaging the dazzling Dennis King, who had created the role of François Villon on Broadway.

Paramount next put her into another Lubitsch picture, MONTE CARLO, costarring with Jack Buchanan. She sang "Beyond the Blue Horizon," which was to become one of her theme songs.

Next came a desert island pot-pourri with numbers, LET'S GO NATIVE.

Now she moved to United Artists for Friml's THE LOTTERY BRIDE, and to Fox to make OH, FOR A MAN.

In the present system of cautious and careful film production, it is interesting to note that in 1930, Jeanette MacDonald made five pictures!

She went on, alternating straight and musical films, including three more with Maurice Chevalier, becoming almost, but not quite, a TEAM. ONE HOUR WITH YOU, LOVE ME TONIGHT (a classic, with a glorious score by Richard

Rodgers and Lorenz Hart), and THE MERRY WIDOW.

Then, in 1935, came the jackpot pairing of Jeanette MacDonald with Nelson Eddy.

(Their paths had crossed, unnoted, in the early twenties. Jeanette MacDonald had left Philadelphia to join her sister, Blossom, in search of a Broadway career. At the same time, Nelson Eddy arrived in Philadelphia to try out for a part in IOLANTHE with a local company. He got the job and stayed in Philadelphia for eight years. Meanwhile, the Philadelphia girl was making her way in New York.)

She had, up to this time, not had a leading man who could match her vocal powers, no one with whom a love duet was possible. Some thought that Nelson Eddy might fill the bill, but nothing came of the idea for some time.

He was an upcoming young singer of the day—almost *too* handsome. Tall and blond and teeth and smile. He had been a member of the aforementioned Savoy Opera Company of Philadelphia, with whom he sang Gilbert and Sullivan leads. This led to AIDA for the Philadelphia Operatic Society and PAGLIACCI for the Civic Opera Company. After six years with this organization, he joined the Philadelphia Grand Opera Society and made his New York debut with them in Alban Berg's WOZZECK.

His attractiveness—in addition to his powerful baritone—made him one of the most popular and sought-after singers of the thirties.

In 1933, he gave a concert in Los Angeles that proved to be an historic success. He captured the imagination, as well as the ears, of the public, which demanded and got eighteen encores.

RKO offered him a screen test. Why it was necessary is a mystery. In any event, RKO failed to exercise its option. Eddy was eventually signed to a stock contract by MGM. His career there began inauspiciously with a small singing role in DANCING LADY with Joan Crawford and Clark Gable. Another bit player in this film was Fred Astaire. Then BROADWAY TO HOLLYWOOD with Alice Brady and Frank Morgan, followed by STUDENT TOUR with Jimmy Durante. Lord, O Lord, how they turned them

out in those frenetic days. There was so much work to do that it left little time for thought. How else to explain the fact that it took over two years for the Metro brass to realize that Jeanette MacDonald and Nelson Eddy could be a TEAM?

Credit for the matchmaking has been grabbed by many and claimed by even more, but the facts do not support anyone.

"The greatest caster in the whole world," said Joe Pasternak, "is God."

In the case of MacDonald and Eddy, this claim is borne out.

Eddy was under contract to MGM when preproduction work began on NAUGHTY MARIETTA, the Victor Herbert perennial which was to star Jeanette MacDonald. Lawrence Tibbett, of the Metropolitan Opera Company, was considered briefly as MacDonald's leading man, but a review of the grosses of the films he had done, ROGUE SONG, NEW MOON, and CUBAN LOVE SONG, soon put an end to the idea.

L. B. Mayer finally decided on Allan Jones, who was at the time under contract to the Shuberts. The Shuberts wanted $50,000 for a release.

"Get your release, and you've got the job," said L. B., never famed for his generosity.

Jones asked if MGM would advance the sum. L. B. considered it too much of a gamble, and in addition, was fearful of legal entanglements with the Shuberts. Negotiations dragged on for weeks. Finally, in desperation, Jones flew to St. Louis, where he had often sung with the Municipal Opera Company. A friend there offered to lend him the sum. Jones now flew to New York, so excited that he forgot to contact MGM, as promised. The studio, assuming that his efforts had failed, reluctantly put Nelson Eddy into the picture. By the time Jones checked in, it was too late. "So I lost the role," he says, "and Jeanette MacDonald and Nelson Eddy became the new love team."

The story may be apocryphal, but it is the gospel according to Jones.

NAUGHTY MARIETTA has a lively, melodious score: "The Italian Street Song," "Tramp,

Naughty Marietta *1935*

Rose-Marie *1936*

Naughty Marietta *1935*

Maytime *1937*

Girl of the Golden West *1938*

Girl of the Golden West *1938*

Tramp, Tramp," "Ah, Sweet Mystery of Life." But it is a tribute to the talents of MacDonald and Eddy that they were able to survive the book. John Lee Mahin and Frances Goodrich and Albert Hackett were brought in to resuscitate the moribund book by Rita Johnson Young. W. S. Van Dyke, one of the studio's aces, was assigned to direct. A strong supporting cast was assembled: Frank Morgan, Elsa Lanchester, Joseph Cawthorn, Akim Tamiroff. Still, no amount of dressing, seasoning, or gravy could make this stale turkey palatable.

Consider the yarn. She is Princess Marie de la Bonfain in the court of Louis XV of France. On the verge of being forced into a loveless political marriage, she runs away. Disguised as her own maid, she offers herself as an auction bride, is bought and sold and sails off to Louisiana Territory. There she encounters *him,* a Yankee scout named Captain Richard Warrington. She falls in love with him, and he with her, even though he does not know that she is etcetera, etcetera, etcetera.

Never mind.

The TEAM clicked. The voices blended. The personalities meshed. And MGM had on its hands one of the most successful TEAMS in the long history of on-screen marriages.

But did the front office recognize at once what they had? They did? Then why did they immediately begin negotiations with Grace Moore—who had made a hit in ONE NIGHT OF LOVE at Columbia—to costar with Nelson Eddy in ROSE-MARIE? Grace Moore turned it down. Eddy, she said, was not "important" enough for her. So it was that ROSE-MARIE became the second MacDonald-Eddy feature. With Hollywood irony, Allan Jones was cast in a supporting role. "Rose-Marie" and "Indian Love Call" were retained from Friml's score. Arias from ROMEO AND JULIET, as well as TOSCA, were interpolated. And since the story concerned Rose-Marie's trek into the wilderness in search of her errant brother and the necessity for her to find employment in a roughneck saloon, Jeanette MacDonald also sang Sophie Tucker's signature song, "Some of These Days," as well as "Dinah" under the tutelage of Gilda Gray,

the former Ziegfeld star, who had created the shimmy.

MGM used to give the folks a lot for their money. As the canny old showman, Charles Taylor, once complained, "They give them *too* much nowadays."

A straight movie for MacDonald followed: SAN FRANCISCO, with Clark Gable and Spencer Tracy.

Then it was back to song and Nelson again with MAYTIME. Not only Nelson Eddy this time, but John Barrymore and the Don Cossack Choir. And Herman Bing, Tom Brown, Paul Porcasi, Sig Rumann, Guy Bates Post, and Billy Gilbert. A sequence from the opera, LES HUGUENOTS, and a created opera, using parts of Tchaikovsky's Fifth Symphony. (Charles Taylor was just damn right.)

MAYTIME proved to be a harrowing ordeal for all concerned. Irving Thalberg, the young movie wizard, was personally supervising the production—and battling his nemesis, L. B. Mayer, daily. L. B. took a puritanical view of every shot in every MGM picture. The sordid details of his private life notwithstanding, he wanted everything on the screen to be clean and neat and sweet and all-American and love-your-mother and apple pie. The very idea—in MAYTIME—of a man and a married woman attracted to each other (even without consummation) drove Mayer wild. He hectored Thalberg continuously. Thalberg, in charge, brushed him aside and went his brilliant way. Until September 14, 1936, when Irving Thalberg died at the age of thirty-seven.

L. B. Mayer immediately closed down the MAYTIME production and took charge. The story and script were revised according to his moral standards.

He thought Richard Wayne a "dirty" name (!). It was changed in Version II to Paul Allison (obviously a "clean" name).

Other names were changed as well—on-screen and off. The director, Edmund Goulding, became Robert Z. Leonard. Paul Lukas to John Barrymore. Frank Morgan to Herman Bing.

I Married an Angel   *1942*

Girl of the Golden West   *1938*

I Married an Angel   *1942*

Naughty Marietta   *1935*

I Married an Angel   *1942*

Bitter Sweet   *1940*

Characters were eliminated, and the footage which had been shot was scrapped. Production began again—this time in black and white. Mayer hated Technicolor. It hurt his eyes, he said.

A further complication. Nelson Eddy had been booked for a forty-three-day concert tour, and it could not be postponed. Thus, all his scenes had to be bunched, making a shambles of the schedule.

But there was no arguing with the Dictator—L. B. Mayer.

The final production was not well received critically, but succeeded because Jeanette MacDonald and Nelson Eddy were flying high. The public loved the TEAM. Inside movie wiseguys made jokes. Ben Hecht dubbed her the Iron Butterfly. And his partner, Charlie MacArthur, not to be outdone, named Eddy "Stainless Steel." The TEAM's reply to these barbs was another smash hit, a curious version of THE GIRL OF THE GOLDEN WEST, and Victor Herbert's SWEETHEARTS.

At this point, Jeanette MacDonald became restive. She told Mayer that she did not want to spend the rest of her professional life as half of a TEAM.

Nelson Eddy, more pragmatic, argued that they had a good thing going, so why not continue with it?

He was to be proved correct, for himself at least. All his other teamings failed. ROSALIE, with Eleanor Powell and Ilona Massey; LET FREEDOM RING, with Virginia Bruce; BALALAIKA, with Ilona Massey; and THE CHOCOLATE SOLDIER, with Risë Stevens.

And although he made many more films, it is only his partnership with Jeanette MacDonald that keeps him firmly fixed in our memories.

Mayer, a skillful manipulator, gave MacDonald a rest, then put her into BROADWAY SERENADE with Lew Ayres, Frank Morgan, and Ian Hunter. A failure.

There are those who say that L. B. deliberately sabotaged the film in order to frighten MacDonald into returning to the safety of MacDonald and Eddy, Inc. Could be.

Maytime *1937*

Rose-Marie *1936*

They were reunited in NEW MOON, the successful Sigmund Romberg show, and continued without complaint into Noel Coward's lovely BITTER SWEET.

By this time, Jeanette MacDonald had married Gene Raymond and insisted upon making a film with him. A third remake of SMILIN' THROUGH was chosen. It had been made as a silent with Norma Talmadge in 1922 and as a talkie with Norma Shearer and Leslie Howard in 1932. Third time unlucky. And so it was back to the MacDonald-Eddy assembly line once more and a botched adaptation of the Rodgers and Hart Broadway musical, I MARRIED AN ANGEL.

In addition to the stunning Rodgers and Hart score, Jeanette MacDonald sang "Clair de Lune," accompanied by fifty harps.

To those who wonder how MGM found fifty harpists in Hollywood, let me relate how I once lost a bet with Buddy De Sylva, who was producing BACHELOR MOTHER, with Ginger Rogers and David Niven, a film I was directing.

When Buddy disapproved of a minor bit of casting I had done, I testily told him that no type could be found to suit the description in the script.

"Banana oil," said Buddy. "This town's got anything and everything. What'll you bet I can have ten blue-eyed guys with broken noses standing right here by ten o'clock tomorrow morning—and the broken noses all pointing *that* way?"

"A hundred bucks," I said.

"You got it."

The next morning at 10:10, I had to pay the bet off.

I MARRIED AN ANGEL proved to be a mistake. The required light fantastic touch was missing.

Moreover, after eight big pictures, the limited resources of the TEAM had apparently been exhausted.

Jeanette MacDonald and Nelson Eddy never worked together again, although they remained the closest of friends until her death in 1965.

Nelson Eddy said, "Many of the friends we worked with at MGM are gone. You accept it. But Jeanette MacDonald . . . you just can't accept it. . . . I'll never get over it."

Two years later, in the midst of a successful nightclub engagement in Miami Beach, Nelson Eddy collapsed and died.

Memories are moments, and one of the most delicious is a scene in ROSE-MARIE:

Jeanette MacDonald, preparing for bed in her boudoir, hears three familiar notes sung in the garden below. She floats out, a cloud of whiteness, onto the balcony—yes, balcony—and looks down into the shadows.

"Who's there?" she calls. (As if she didn't know.)

Reverse shot from her angle. Nelson Eddy. He salutes and says, "Your dream prince, reporting for duty!"

Oh, where are the snowjobs of yesteryear?

Blockheads 1938

Another Fine Mess
LAUREL and HARDY

The distinguished British film critic, Miss Dilys Powell, and I once quarreled amiably about the talents of a young British comedian named Norman Wisdom. I found him hilarious, inventive, touching, appealing, and dared to think he might easily develop into one of Britain's great comedians.

Dilys disagreed and said, somewhat didactically, "No, no, Norman is bright and funny, but he has no future."

"Why not?" I asked.

"Because," she said very simply, "he lacks elegance."

I was not sure what she meant, but as time went by, I was able to perceive the accuracy of her estimate. It is perfectly true that all the great comedians have elegance or something very like it. Charlie Chaplin, Buster Keaton, Harry Langdon, Harold Lloyd, Ed Wynn, Bert Lahr, Phil Silvers, Danny Kaye, Zero Mostel, the Marx Brothers, Max Linder.

And then, to make the point, think of the comedians who do not have it: Jerry Lewis, Milton Berle, Henny Youngman, Don Rickles —successful, yes; elegant, no.

Prime masters in the art of elegance are Laurel and Hardy.

(How easily the present tense flows from one's pen when discussing immortals. Stan is gone. Babe is no more. And yet the wonders and the art of Laurel and Hardy remain for all time in the manner of great painting, poetry, and literature.)

Both of them moved with astonishing grace, and what is even more important in the case of comedy, with rhythm. Moreover, their complex and original and effective individual rhythms had a way of blending to create a marvelous jazz effect.

Much has been said about TEAMS being composed of a male and a female element. A dominating and a dominated. An active and a passive. A conqueror, a conquered.

In every one of their 104 films, it is perfectly clear that Ollie is the strong one, and Stan, the weak. The catchphrase—"*Another fine mess you've got us into!*"—is most certainly characteristic of the patriarch.

What makes this observation especially in-teresting is the knowledge that this relationship was completely reversed in the off-screen life of Laurel and Hardy. Ollie was the passive one, Stan the active. Stan was the director, Ollie the obedient, malleable player. Hardy himself was swift to admit that Laurel was the dominating force of the TEAM and of its work. Whenever a question came up about anything to do with the business of the TEAM, the work of the TEAM, the public relations, the choice of stories, the casting of their supporting players, Ollie had a standard two-word reply: "Ask Stan."

This proves, if further proof is needed, that these two men were consummate actors. Stan Laurel, organizing, inventing, dominating, steps before the camera, and as it begins to roll, changes personality completely to the put-upon schnook, the ineffectual bumbler, the pushed-around patsy.

Ollie, on the other hand, off-screen the somewhat vague, ineffectual creature, becomes the strong protagonist.

Thornton Wilder once said that an artist must be "a flowing cornucopia of ideas, inventions, audacities, notions, and originalities." This, indeed, Laurel and Hardy are. Their collected works represent about half a million feet of film, and I daresay that there is scarcely a foot of it that does not yield some piece of extraordinary comic creation or invention.

They are piano movers. Getting the piano off the truck furnishes a routine for countless details, each one of which is calculated to make us howl with laughter, and does. Being Laurel and Hardy, representing the human race against the forces of nature and civilization, when they get the piano off the truck and check the address, they find that the house to which they are to deliver the piano stands atop a hill reachable only by a long, long, rickety wooden set of outdoor stairs. Since they are piano movers, it is their job to proceed. They do so, creating hysteria every step of the way. And when they reach the top, we know that something more is going to happen. But what? Is the piano going to slip down of its own accord and smash? Is it going to turn out that

Way Out West   *1936*

Hog Wild   *1930*

there is no one home? Or have they got the wrong address? Think of the choices open to them. The one they choose is not the one calculated to raise the loudest gales of laughter, but the one that is most real, most logical, most believable. There is no one home.

Reality is at the core of their comedy. There is hardly ever anything that strains credibility. There are very few coincidences. Once the original theme and key have been established, everything proceeds with frenzied logic.

Laurel and Hardy are illustrious for many things, but nothing more impressive than the brilliance with which they moved from silent films into sound films.

The switch virtually wiped out a whole generation of talents.

No serious film scholar will dispute the assertion that Charlie Chaplin is the single greatest figure to be developed by the medium in its eighty-year history. Yet no knowledgeable observer can take the position that the Chaplin of the talkies approached the genius of the silents. All of them—Chaplin, Harold Lloyd, Buster Keaton, Harry Langdon, Charlie Chase, Lloyd Hamilton, Fatty Arbuckle, Max Linder, Ford Sterling, Hank Mann, Chester Conklin, Billy Bevan, Snub Pollard, Clyde Cook, Jimmy Finlayson, Larry Semon, Lupino Lane, Ben Turpin, Raymond Griffith, Harry Myers—were master mimes. They had to be. The medium in which they were working was silent, and characters, as well as situations, had to be conveyed through movement and expressions alone.

It is true that there was later a development of titles—interspersed lines of description—"DEAD CENTER, MINNESOTA, A TOWN OF 8,420 SOULS." Next card: "4,000 MEN—4,419 WOMEN." Next card: "AND CONRAD HOSENFEFFER." Or sometimes dialogue— "I DID NOT CALL YOU A LIAR—I JUST SAID THAT YOU HANDLE THE TRUTH CARELESSLY!"

But the magic of silent films did not lie in the titles, either the descriptive ones or the dialogue ones. It was all in the pictures, the movement, the choreography, the expression, the body language, the close-ups, the action, the imagery.

With the coming of sound, a new dimension was required. It was as though a successful pianist was told that pianos were to be no more, that if he wanted to continue a concert career, he would have to learn to play the violin. Most of those who attempted the transition failed. Buster Keaton doggedly remained a pantomimist, but no longer a star. Chaplin toyed with the idea of playing a deaf mute, and for a time, in the face of the talkies, persistently stuck to silent pictures. But he was Chaplin, the nonesuch, the nonpareil, the great one. Since he owned his own studio and financed his own films, he could do what he liked. But even he had to succumb in time, and the results, although stunning and inventive and wonderful to watch, fell short of the great work he had done in the silents.

Laurel and Hardy made it. They were not only serious comedians, but serious men, scholars, and artists. In 1928, they made ten pictures. LEAVE 'EM LAUGHING, FROM SOUP TO NUTS, YOU'RE DARN TOOTIN', THEIR PURPLE MOMENTS, SHOULD MARRIED MEN GO HOME?, HABEAS CORPUS, TWO TARS, WE FAW DOWN, THE FINISHING TOUCH, and EARLY TO BED. In 1929, they began with LIBERTY, then took a deep breath and plunged into sound with UNACCUSTOMED AS WE ARE. It turned out surprisingly well. Greatly encouraged, they went on in 1929 to make twelve more sound movies (a total of thirteen for the year!) : DOUBLE WHOOPEE!, BIG BUSINESS, MEN O' WAR, THE PERFECT DAY, ANGORA LOVE, BACON GRABBERS, THEY GO BOOM, THE HOOSEGOW, HOLLYWOOD REVIEW OF 1929 (their first feature-length picture), BERTH MARKS, WRONGED AGAIN, and THAT'S MY WIFE.

Their work with words improved with every picture. Stan was responsible for a good deal of the dialogue, and there is one exchange in their picture called HELPMATES that reveals his understanding of wit.

Ollie asks, "You never met my wife, did you?"

Stan replies, "Yes, I never did."

Only someone whose ear is attuned to comic language could have come up with such a simple but elegant little joke.

Oliver Hardy had an unusually perceptive understanding of his own comic creations: "I'm the dumbest kind of guy there is," he explained. "I'm the dumb guy who thinks he's smart."

There are many Laurel and Hardy aficionados who consider their picture THE BATTLE OF THE CENTURY, one of their films made in 1927, the greatest of all Laurel and Hardys.

Henry Miller has written about it: "And after thousands of slapstick, pie-throwing Mack Sennett films, after Charlie Chaplin had exhausted his bag of tricks, after Fatty Arbuckle, Harold Lloyd, Harry Langdon, Buster Keaton, each with his own special brand of monkeyshines, came the chef d'oeuvre of all the slapstick pie-throwing festivals, the film the very title of which I forget, but it was among the very first films starring Laurel and Hardy.

"This, in my opinion, is the greatest comic film ever made—because it brought the pie throwing to apotheosis. There was nothing but pie throwing in it. Nothing but pies, thousands and thousands of pies, and everybody throwing them right and left. It was the ultimate in burlesque and it is already forgotten."

Stan Laurel's account of the making of that little classic as related to John McCabe:

"For some good reason that I can't think of at the moment, we decided that this should be a fight picture, and for that reason and because of the gigantic pie conflict in it, we called it *The Battle of the Century*. Hardy is my manager. I am a prizefighter. A packed arena. I come out for the first round and get knocked out cold with one blow. Fade out. Fade in. The arena again, only now it is completely empty. I am still out on the deck. Hardy is leaning on ringside, looking into the camera and showing plenty of weariness. Fade out. Next day we're sitting on a park bench, looking miserable. A guy passing us (played by Eugene Palette) is an insurance agent and he suggests to Hardy that he should take out an insurance policy on me as I am very likely to get hurt, and that means money in the bank. It's a cut-rate insurance company he owns. The company gives five hundred dollars at a two-buck fee for a single broken leg or arm. Hardy borrows the two dollars from *me* and pays up. (Hardy has taken

the guy aside so I can't hear any of this.) Hardy then takes me for a walk around town, trying various methods to get me in an accident. He walks me under ladders where construction is going on and he gets conked instead. He passes a fruit stand and buys a banana. As we are walking along, he peels it and throws the skin in front of me so that I'll slip on it. I, unknowingly, step over it. He picks it up, drops it in back of him and leads me around to walk on it again, and of course, he slips on it and crashes to the ground. We come to a bakery shop with a pie wagon standing in front. Hardy drops the peel for me on the sidewalk there and the pie man comes along with a big tray of pies and slips on the peel. He's covered with pies. As he clears his eyes, he happens to see Hardy pushing the banana into my hand and realizes that Hardy is trying to put the blame on me. An argument starts, ending up with the pie man pushing a pie in Hardy's face. I resent this and push a pie in the pie man's face. Hardy laughs at this, and the guy, instead of hitting me back, hits Hardy with another pie. At this point, a stranger passing by tries to stop the argument and he gets the pie in the face too. Gradually, one by one, other people get into the argument, until finally the entire street, the full block, is pie crazy. Everybody is pie-throwing happy. The camera goes up to take a panorama view of all these people throwing, throwing, throwing. There are pies thrown into a dentist's office, in windows, out of them, nothing but pies, thousands of them. Then a cop, who of course is all covered with pie, arrests us and is taking us away when he slips on the banana peel and he falls down a manhole for the finish."

It is interesting to note that the idea of the pie in the face had become a movie cliché by this time. Stale and old-fashioned. But Stan Laurel thought there was one more great turn to be wrung on it. He said to the staff, "Let's make a pie picture to end all pie pictures. Let's give them so many pies that there will never be room for any more pie pictures in the whole history of the movies."

And that is precisely what they did. They used literally thousands of pies. By now no one

Liberty *1929*

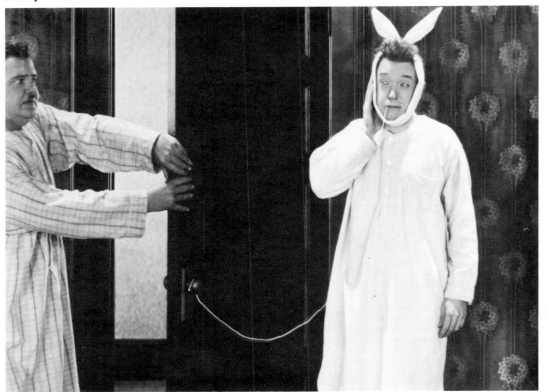

Leave Em Laughing *1928*

can remember the exact number. Estimates range anywhere from three thousand pies to ten thousand pies. Moreover, they were real pies, custard pies, cherry pies, coconut pies, banana, lemon meringue, blueberry, raspberry. The entire stock of the Los Angeles Pie Company was bought by the property man and used. Talk about the theory of conspicuous waste! Still, no one who ever saw THE BATTLE OF THE CENTURY is likely to forget it.

Stan Laurel on the subject of production: "We had a rough idea of schedules, but our prime worry was whether or not the picture was going to be good. The studio didn't bother us much, if at all, about a schedule because we didn't have a lot of people in our cast, as a rule. There weren't any unions, and people just worked until we got the effects we wanted. Sometimes we would have a change in a gag situation that called for alterations in the set. So we'd wait a couple of days until it was rebuilt. That takes time. We really didn't have any idea of how precisely long it would take us to do a film. It really depended on the kind we were doing. If we were doing both day and night exterior shots on the same set, we would sometimes keep going right through the day and then on all that night until the following morning. This, of course, when we felt like going ahead on a spurt to finish the picture. It got pretty rough at times, especially if we were making water scenes. You can get pretty tired working all night soaking wet, as we did on many occasions. As for the times between pictures, that always varied. After the picture was assembled, we previewed it, and if no retakes were needed, we started to prepare the next story. That would generally take three or four weeks, sometimes more, sometimes less. Years later, more time was taken on feature films, of course. If [Hal] Roach was anxious for us to get started, we'd go into production almost right away after finishing a picture and complete the script as we went along. We would start out with an idea, go along working on it as we were shooting, and then we would frequently deviate from the original idea. We worked hard, but there was no real pressure.

It was fun, particularly in the silent days. If something went wrong with what we were doing, we'd just 'cut' and laugh about it. Then we'd talk it over and go on shooting. It was damned fine fun and damned hard work in those days when we were making ourselves a well-known team. Come to think of it, it was always fun."

A hallmark of the work of Laurel and Hardy is its variety and versatility. Having established a character for each of them and a relationship, they now used the structure in countless ways. They were eager parodists, and when the Rudolph Valentino picture called BLOOD AND SAND was released, they immediately came up with MUD AND SAND, in which Stan Laurel played a sheik called Rubarb Vaselino. When a successful version of ROBIN HOOD was done, they lost no time producing ROB 'EM GOOD. Later came a period piece called WHEN KNIGHTS WERE BOLD. The Laurel and Hardy version was called WHEN KNIGHTS WERE COLD. In the course of their work, they played Foreign Legionnaires, piano movers, college students, sailors, soldiers, insurance salesmen, crooks, cops, dog catchers, playboys, bums, prizefighters, detectives, convicts, bullfighters, Scotsmen, magicians, bathhouse attendants, tailors, streetcar conductors, carpenters, house painters, big businessmen.

In fact, there is scarcely an area of human activity that they did not cover and comment upon in a sage and remarkable manner.

But, thank Fortune, whatever they played, in whatever period or costume or character, they were always firmly Laurel and Hardy, and we accepted them gratefully and happily.

It was an astonishing feat to be able to place these characters in any chosen situation or set of circumstances. Laurel and Hardy are, in fact, among the great comic creations, along with Sganarelle or Pierrot and Columbine or, for that matter, Punch and Judy.

So vast is the oeuvre of Laurel and Hardy that no single collector of Laurel and Hardy films—and there are a great many such collectors—has a complete set. No film collection or archives makes such a claim. But there is, some here and there—at the Cinémathèque Française in Paris, at the American Film Institute, at the Academy of Motion Picture Arts and Sciences, as well as in private collections—one of the most astonishing and valuable and useful comic creations of all time, and for all time, as well.

The Laurel and Hardy library preserved reminds us once again of the value of such work and the importance of preserving it.

Had film been available for a longer period of time than a mere eighty years or so, we would doubtless today be able to see the comic creations of Richard Burbage, Joseph Jefferson, and—imagine it—even the great Molière himself playing TARTUFFE or SCHOOL FOR WIVES. Indeed, we would be able to see William Shakespeare and Johann Nestroy and the whole long line of that most sainted breed, the clown.

Speaking for myself, I cannot like anyone who does not like Laurel and Hardy, nor love anyone who does not love them.

In 104 films they never ran out of comic ideas, insane invention, charming conceits.

It is in no way surprising that they are the graven images set on a double plinth, before which the most passionately devoted group of cultists in the movie world worships. They call themselves the Sons of the Desert (after a Laurel and Hardy masterpiece), number chapters or "tents" in more than a dozen cities.

In Paris, cinéastes count on the annual two-month Laurel and Hardy Festival.

Stalin, Churchill, and Tito formed an oddly assorted fan club who regularly held showings of their Laurel and Hardy collections.

Oliver Hardy was an American southern gentleman, an expert golfer despite his 350 pounds. Stan Laurel was a low-born Lancashire cockney, who had once understudied Charlie Chaplin. Their off-screen lives were as different as their sizes and shapes.

"Ollie and I had different hobbies," Stan once told an interviewer. "He liked horses and golf. You know *my* hobby—and I married them all."

In point of fact, Stan Laurel's domestic life was every bit as daffy as the character he played. He married four women eight times: Lois Nielson, Virginia Ruth Rogers, Vera Illeana, and Ida Kitaeva Raphael, and successfully defended a suit by a fifth, Mae Laurel, who claimed to have been his common-law wife.

The TEAM was formed comparatively late in life and career for both. The year was 1927. Laurel was thirty-seven; Hardy thirty-five.

Laurel, after a mildly successful run as a screen comedian for Broncho Billy and Hal Roach, gave it up to become a director. In due time, he was directing one of Hal Roach's All Star Series with Hardy playing the lead, a timid butler, in a film called GET 'EM YOUNG. A few days after shooting began, Hardy, a gourmet cook, burned his arm badly while cooking a leg of lamb and had to withdraw. In the sausage-factory assembly-line methods of the day, Laurel was compelled to step in as a substitute. Hardy recovered, returned, and Roach, as a matter of economy, insisted they both stay in the film. Laurel agreed reluctantly. That did it. A hundred and four films later, they were still together—and never acted without each other.

Listen to these two celebrated "dopes" discuss comedy:

Hardy: "The fun is in the story situations which make an audience sorry for the comedian. A funny man has to make himself inferior."

Laurel: "Let a fellow try to outsmart his audience, and he misses. It's human nature to laugh at a bird who gets a bucket of paint smeared on his face—even though it makes him miserable."

Hardy: "A comedian has to knock dignity off the pedestal. He has to look small—even I do—by a mental comparison. Lean or fat, short or tall, he has to be pitied to be laughed at."

Laurel: "Sometimes we even feel sorry for each other. That always gets a laugh out of me, when I can feel sorry for Babe."

Hardy: "Me, too. When I can feel sorry for Stan."

48

Stan Laurel (in front) and Oliver Hardy

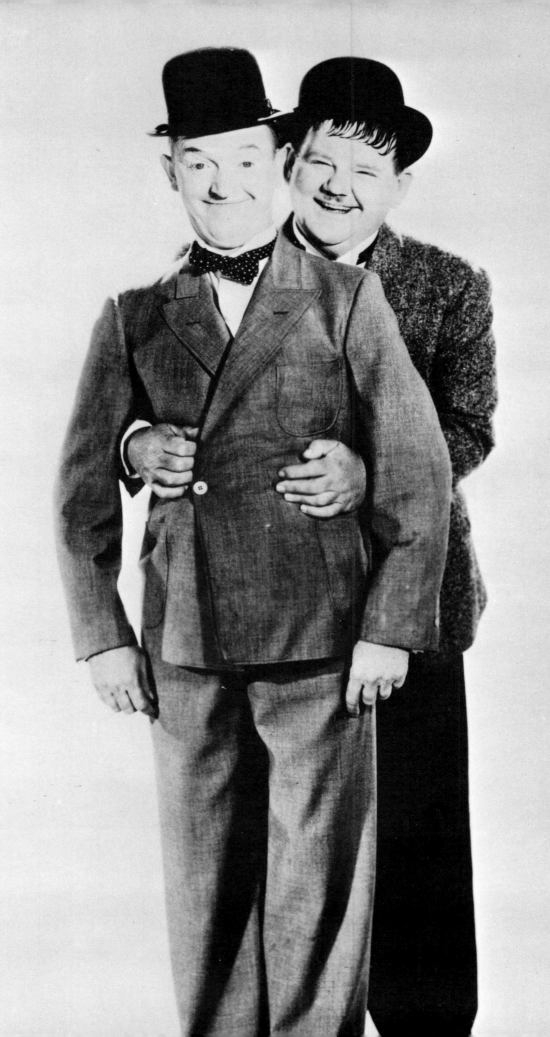

The TEAM was formed comparatively late
in life and career for both.
The year was 1927. Laurel was 37; Hardy, 35...

A hundred and four films later, they were still together—and never acted without each other.

Did anyone ever throw a pie in the face before Laurel and Hardy? I doubt it. But so easy was the bit and so sure-fire the effect that it was immediately stolen and copied by all.

A fat guy and a skinny guy would appear to be traditional in the world of comedy TEAMS: Don Quixote and Sancho Panza, Sir Toby Belch and Andrew Aguecheek, Mutt and Jeff, Weber and Fields, and so on. This pattern was what Hal Roach had in mind when he created the partnership. But I submit that these two superlative comic inventors would have succeeded had they both been fat, both thin, or both in between.

Consider but a few of the titles of their 104 films—do they not indicate what is in store for the lucky young buff who begins to discover the joy of Laurel and Hardy? PARDON US, PACK UP YOUR TROUBLES, THE DEVIL'S BROTHER, SONS OF THE DESERT, HOLLYWOOD PARTY, OUR RELATIONS, WAY OUT WEST, SWISS MISS, BLOCKHEADS, A CHUMP AT OXFORD, AIR RAID WARDENS, JITTERBUGS, THE BULLFIGHTERS.

Hardy was "Ollie" on the screen, but "Babe" to his friends. Why Babe? Let him explain how it happened:

"A fairy Italian barber did it. He had a thick accent, and he liked boys. Well, he took a great fancy to me, and every time after he'd finish shaving me, he'd rub powder into my face and pat my cheeks and say, 'Nice-a Bab-ee. Nice-a Babee.' The gang always used to kid me about it, and after a while they started to call me Baby, and then it was cut down to Babe—and I've been Babe Hardy ever since—but never a fairy!"

The joint career of Laurel and Hardy peaked in the thirties, then faded slowly and sadly. The art had become an industry; the players had become properties. The Master Minds had taken over. This was not the climate in which Mr. Elf and Mr. Sprite could function. The later pictures failed. Still, their public did not desert them. They made personal-appearance tours all over the world with enormous success. In Glasgow, thirty people were hospitalized as a result of the rush to see them. In France, the President of the Republic sent his car to carry them in a motorcade down the Champs Élysées. In Cobh, Ireland, whistles blew, blasts sounded, and thousands on the dock cheered as their ship landed. Stan recalls it thus:

"Our last good pictures were made in the thirties, and you'd think people would forget, but they don't. We just couldn't understand what it was all about. And then something happened that I can never forget. All the church bells in Cobh started to ring out our theme song—The Cuckoo Song—and Babe looked at me, and we cried. . . . I'll never forget that day. Never."

After the Thin Man *1936*

The Sophisticates
WILLIAM POWELL and MYRNA LOY

Together, they represented the ultimate in enviable urbanity, charming wickedness, marital bliss, and sophisticated sex.

That was the illusion. The reality was something else again.

Myrna Williams was born in Raidersburg, Montana, on August 2, 1905. She found her way to Hollywood early on and made her film debut at nineteen in an MGM program picture called PRETTY LADIES. (A prophetic title. In 1981, at the age of seventy-six, Myrna Loy is still, indubitably, a mighty pretty lady, indeed!) The shape of her wondrous sloe eyes determined the shape of her early career. The well-bred, nice girl from Montana was metamorphosed into all manner of Orientals and gypsies and primitive and foreign temptresses and Mideastern princesses and mysterious femmes fatales who spoke no known language and did it all with their sloe eyes. A few of her early films: BEN HUR, THE CAVE MAN, DON JUAN, NOAH'S ARK, THE DESERT SONG, THE SQUALL.

She was soon in great demand, and in 1927 acted in no fewer than eleven different movies —all for Warner Brothers, to whom she was under contract. The boys got their money's worth in those days.

In her first decade as a film actress, Myrna Loy made seventy-six pictures, and she was not yet thirty. The very bulk of the work provided an incomparable training ground. She played opposite virtually every star of the period—learning, experimenting, developing. Once under contract, there was less and less type-casting. Contract players were used for anything available. The idea was to keep them steadily employed. "You're getting paid, aren't you?"

In 1934, David O. Selznick, then a producer at Metro, put together one of the studio's "big" pictures of the year, MANHATTAN MELODRAMA. It was not terribly Manhattan, being shot almost entirely on the back lot, with a few stock shots of New York dropped in like raisins into the rice pudding; but it sure was Melodrama. Two boys from New York's Hell's Kitchen lose their parents when a riverboat is lost. One of them, Blackie Gallagher (played by Mickey Rooney), grows up to be a gambler, a gangster, an all-round low-life (played by Clark Gable). The other, Jim Wade (played by Jimmy Butler), becomes (have you got it yet?) a New York City district attorney (played by William Powell). In spite of their respective positions, they remain friends of a sort.

Blackie has a girlfriend, Eleanor (no last name)—Loy's part—who is clearly his mistress, although the word is never uttered in the film.

When Blackie is too involved in monkey-shines to attend a dinner for his pal, Jim, he sends Eleanor as a stand-in.

This is how Powell and Loy meet (on-screen, at any rate), and a TEAM is born. The style that was to serve them so well for the next thirteen years was born in the very first scene they played together. They are sharing a taxi. They have never met before. We see at once that they are magnetically attracted to one another, despite the fact that they know they should not be. Blackie, after all, stands between them—to say nothing of Clark Gable. But they make love with words—expensive words provided by a crack Metro team composed of Arthur Caesar, Oliver T. Marsh, H. P. Garrett, and Joseph L. Mankiewicz.

ELEANOR/LOY
Nothing like a district attorney to keep a girl in shape.
(Up goes Jim/Powell's eyebrow)
We must have a good wrestle some day.

(A few minutes later, he demonstrates that he can show off as well as she can, as he tells her the story of his life)

JIM/POWELL
I was born at home because I wanted to be near mother.

All delivered with the kind of elegance generally reserved for the highest sort of high comedy.

In time, she resigns as Blackie's mistress and signs on as Jim's wife. (Yes, it *is* a long story, but remember, it had four writers on it.)

Blackie winds up in the electric chair; Jim, a civilian again, with Eleanor at his side.

A few weeks after MANHATTAN MELODRAMA completed shooting, a "small" picture was rushed into production—THE THIN MAN, from the novel by Dashiell Hammett. With uncharacteristic sagacity, the front office had assigned the husband-wife writing team of Frances Goodrich and Albert Hackett to the screenplay. The Hacketts were close friends of Hammett and thus were able to preserve and maintain his style.

William Powell's permanent image was formed with this picture—made in fifteen days by W. S. Van Dyke, who had also directed MANHATTAN MELODRAMA. It was an over-the-moon triumph.

Bill Powell had come a long way from Pittsburgh, Pennsylvania, where he was born on July 29, 1892.

To be an actor was his earliest ambition, and it led him to New York and the American Academy of Dramatic Arts. Upon graduation, he began the usual struggle for recognition, without conspicuous success. World War I and the Army. Upon his discharge, disillusioned with the theatre which had failed him, he went to Hollywood and became a heavy in westerns, sometimes acting under pseudonyms. In 1922, a break at last. Signed by Samuel Goldwyn to play in SHERLOCK HOLMES. From that point on, his career picked up steam. WHEN KNIGHTHOOD WAS IN FLOWER, UNDER THE RED ROBE, to Italy with the Gish sisters for ROMOLA, which led to a long-term contract, Paramount, and stardom.

Among the many films he made there were those in the Philo Vance detective series, and so strong was his association with that role that when he was married to Carole Lombard, she never called him anything but Philo.

It was this that led the MGM brass to cast him as Nick Charles in THE THIN MAN, and it was the positive chemistry exuded by Powell and Loy in MANHATTAN MELODRAMA that got her the assignment. How Asta got in there, no one knows.

What Powell and Loy did was—and no mean feat—to make marriage fun, not to make fun of marriage. No formula here, no boy-meets-girl, boy-loses-girl, boy-gets-girl. It was more like man-has-wife, man-has-wife, man-has-

wife. And happily. And joyously.

Dashiell Hammett and Lillian Hellman are the prototypes for Nick and Nora Charles. Powell, not a bit like Hammett in person, nor Loy like Hellman, yet the spirit is there. The sense of life's excitement and unpredictability and terror and gaiety.

Had Metro had any idea that THE THIN MAN would be such a smash, they would surely have had a sequel ready to follow. As it happened, two years were to pass before Hunt Stromberg could arrange the second of the series. One of Hollywood's most astute producers, he persuaded Dashiell Hammett himself to provide a story and engaged Goodrich and Hackett to do the screenplay.

Meanwhile, the TEAM—not to be separated—was cast in EVELYN PRENTICE, a melodrama that made MANHATTAN MELODRAMA look like a farce. Adultery, blackmail, homicide, false accusation, confession, double-bullet murder dénouement.

THE THIN MAN sequel still in work, our TEAM was cast in the MGM extravaganza, THE GREAT ZIEGFELD—with William Powell as Florenz Ziegfeld and Myrna Loy as his wife, Billie Burke.

(Billie Burke once told me that her husband had actually been christened "Florence," and only later in life, when bearing a girl's name became an unwieldy embarrassment, did he replace the "ce" with a "z." She showed me their marriage certificate: Florence Ziegfeld and Billie Burke. Talk about role reversal!)

The TEAM was buried under the massive "production values." Moreover, both were badly miscast—still the film itself won the Academy Award as Best Picture.

LIBELED LADY came next. In those days of block booking, a few surefire smashes on which to hang the rest of their program were needed by every studio. When the screenplay of LIBELED LADY proved to have in it four good roles, it was decided to "cast it up." The result was a film starring Spencer Tracy, William Powell, Jean Harlow, and Myrna Loy—any *one* of whom could have carried a picture at that time.

What is more important is the fact that LIBELED LADY turned out to be one of the five or six funniest comedies ever made in Hollywood. An out-and-out knockout.

Now at last: AFTER THE THIN MAN. All concerned were aware that if this could top the first, a series might be in order—if it flopped, it was all over. No time, no expense was spared. The effort paid off—and the tag promised still another THIN MAN. A San Francisco to New York luxury train—the Pacific Flyer. Nora is sitting in a drawing room, knitting a tiny baby sweater. Nick comes in, looks at it, at her, at it, at her. "And you call yourself a detective," she says. Fade out. It tells us that, of course, there will be another.

But first, DOUBLE WEDDING, a somewhat derivative screwball comedy—of the sort then in vogue. It failed, and the studio swiftly returned to safer ground.

ANOTHER THIN MAN, with a screenplay this time by Dashiell Hammett himself. The baby (Nick, Jr.) was indeed in it—but the notion was beginning to pale.

The TEAM made I LOVE YOU AGAIN—and a great success. The Hollywood roller coaster in frenetic action.

Still another screwball comedy came next, LOVE CRAZY, which some Powell-Loy experts believe to be the apex of their teamwork.

But exhibitors and distributors, to say nothing of the public, were clamoring for still another THIN MAN, and the studio obliged with SHADOW OF THE THIN MAN.

By this time, only a few of Hammett's characters were being used. The story was by Harry Kurnitz, screenplay by Harry Kurnitz and Irving Brecher.

It was the first THIN MAN failure. MGM released it on a saturation booking to kill the word of mouth—and it played in 410 theatres during Thanksgiving week, 1941.

Three years later—THE THIN MAN GOES HOME. A formidable writing team went to work. Story by Harry Kurnitz and Robert Riskin. Screenplay by Robert Riskin and Dwight Taylor (the brilliant son of Laurette).

Woody Van Dyke was dead. Thus the TEAM had to have a new director—Richard Thorpe. The result was a fair-to-middling wartime success.

The Great Ziegfeld   *1936*

After the Thin Man   *1936*

The Thin Man   *1934*

Double Wedding   *1937*

Three more years—then the last of the THIN MAN series, and alas, the worst: SONG OF THE THIN MAN.

Inspiration flagged, it was a sixth carbon copy, barely readable.

The same year, Powell went to Universal to make a movie with Nunnally Johnson and Charlie MacArthur and George S. Kaufman, THE SENATOR WAS INDISCREET. Myrna Loy loyally turned up to play a bit part in the trick ending.

The TEAM had had it and was gone forever. But what memories of it remain!

William Powell and Myrna Loy admired one another as persons and as players. Here she is categorizing her erstwhile partner and friend, at the request of a fan magazine: "If Bill were a drink, he'd be a potent-looking cocktail in a tall, narrow glass of fine crystal. The stuff in it would be as potent as you thought it would be, too. . . . In literature, he suggests Noel Coward, much of Saki, some of Oscar Wilde's epigrams; lately, the Book of Job it would seem; a work on economics, some Schopenhauer, and a history of acting. . . . As to sports and games: something performed indoors, certainly, since Bill loathes exercise. Contract bridge played lying down with automatic thingamies to shuffle and deal. Table tennis with a proxy for Bill. . . . Two of the most important things about Bill Powell are his ability as an actor and his sense of humor, which are unfailing, often biting, always objective. With all the outward manifestations of a lazy, luxurious person, he is essentially a vital, supremely intelligent man."

Turnabout being fair play, let us hear from William Powell about Myrna Loy:

"Conjure Myrna into an automobile and I think you get an open Phaeton, smart and sporty but with plenty of room for the family. The machine would be decorated with many horns and gadgets, it would have a conservative paint job, but it would go like the dickens when pressed on the accelerator, the while scrupulously observant of all and any traffic regulations. One would notice such a car if it were parked along a curb and it would be fun to own, still it would be comfortable for long rides. . . . She is a willow tree, graceful and

Libeled Lady   *1936*

Libeled Lady   *1936*

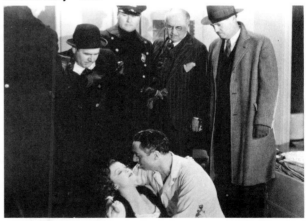

The Thin Man   *1934*

63   Double Wedding   *1937*

The Thin Man   *1934*

After the Thin Man   *1936*

Double Wedding   *1937*

After the Thin Man   *1936*

Publicity shot

I Love You Again   *1940*

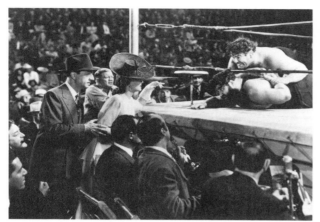

Shadow of the Thin Man   *1941*

After the Thin Man (*with Sam Levine*)   *1936*

Another Thin Man   *1939*

Another Thin Man   *1939*

I Love You Again   *1940*

After the Thin Man   *1936*

I Love You Again   *1940*

After the Thin Man   *1936*

pretty. This must be qualified. Under the branches, a bunch of neighborhood kids have built some sort of shack and would be playing Mr. and Mrs. without fear of interruption. So coy somehow, trying to describe Mrs. Charles in terms of domestic flora. If I say willow, I imply the drooping, whimsical personality which has no relationship to Loy as I know her. If I say an oleander, you know only that I remember an oleander is lovely and my imagination must be very tired. Let her be any healthy tree that doesn't demand attention all the time, but possesses trim lines and nice green leaves and an all-year-round stability of beauty. . . . Her poise is fantastic. It's unbelievable that anyone could work as hard as she does, be on her toes always, accomplish things with dispatch and efficiency, buck the exhausting nervous strain of stardom and still—through it all maintain such quiet, assured calm. . . . I think the secret may lie in the fact that she combines what is worth surviving in the old fashioned concept with a purely modern, realistic set of ideas. She is ineffably American in that respect. . . . Her charm is that she never tries too hard. She is what she is; her freckles are honest, and so is her appraisal of herself. What she possesses, she exploits. What she does not possess, she does not claim for herself. . . . That's the nicest thing I can say about anyone."

A girl from Montana and a boy from Pittsburgh grew up to become a woman and a man who epitomized urbane sophistication. America.

She grew to be the movies' "perfect wife"; he the archetypical patriarch.

After brilliant careers singly and in tandem, William Powell quietly went into contented retirement and Myrna Loy into *anti*-retirement, becoming a splendid stage actress, and serving in an official capacity for the United States at the United Nations.

But, oh, for the days of Nick and Nora! And Asta.

Babes on Broadway   *1942*

The Boy-Girl Number
MICKEY ROONEY and JUDY GARLAND

By the time Joe Yule, Junior, and Frances Ethel Gumm met, he was Mickey Rooney and she was Judy Garland.

It is difficult—no, impossible—to name two people with more theatrical equipment than these two undersized, overtalented children.

Both had become professionals in their early childhood; Frances, as part of the Gumm Sisters Trio, at the age of two-and-a-half.

She recalled: "My mother told me to sit quietly in a box, but she should have known better. The minute my sisters went on, I marched right out onto the stage. Whatever they were singing I've forgotten, but I paid no attention anyhow and launched into 'Jingle Bells,' the only song in my repertoire. I sang five straight choruses before Daddy carried me off the stage. But from then on, I was part of the family act."

On another occasion she said, not without bitterness: "Either it was go on and perform or get wrapped around a bedpost."

Life was eating and sleeping and traveling and singing and dancing.

The traveling led in time to Lake Tahoe Lodge, where MGM's Billy (Square Deal) Grady was vacationing. In order to be able to declare the holiday a business expense, he signed little Miss Gumm to a stock contract and sent her off to Culver City.

Elsewhere, another vaudeville family, Joe Yule and Nell Carter, was making the third-rate rounds with an infant son, Joe Yule, Junior.

In later years, Mickey used to tease Judy, calling her "Judy-come-lately," who waited two and a half years before making a debut. His own, he claimed, came at the age of eleven months, dressed in a tiny tuxedo.

His first job away from the family act was as a last-minute replacement for a midget named Heinie Hanley, in Chicago, in a play called MR. IRON CLAW.

Then Broadway, when a manager who needed a midget for a play entitled NOT TO BE TRUSTED recalled having heard of a three-year-old monster who had played a midget successfully in Chicago. Joe Junior, succeeded in getting the job, but the play failed.

Another play. Another midget. (Children came cheaper than midgets.) ORCHIDS AND ERMINE. The action required the four-year-old to hold a big black cigar in his mouth all through the play. It ran for six months, and cost Joe Junior, four front teeth.

Nell Carter and Joe Senior, had separated by this time. Joe Junior, needed teeth, but then there were no midget parts in the offing.

Harry Bestry, the agent, finally came to Nell and said, "Nell, I hate to break your heart, but your son is washed up. He's through. He ain't got a chance."

Nell went home and broke the news to Joe Junior. The two troupers wept all night. Joe Junior had yet to celebrate his fifth birthday.

In those days, all show business roads led to Hollywood. There the formidable Max Reinhardt was putting together a stage production of Shakespeare's A MIDSUMMER NIGHT'S DREAM and wanted a child to play Puck. Hundreds were auditioned. Mickey Rooney, as he was now known, got the part.

"I was great," he recalls. "I didn't know what the hell the Kraut was talking about. And I didn't understand what *I* was talking about either. But I was great. *Great!*"

Others thought so, too. Mickey found himself under contract as a stock player at MGM.

It was only natural that the two teenagers should become chums. They entertained at studio parties, in the commissary, in projection rooms, in the barber shop, in the makeup department, and out on the driveways.

Judy had played bits in EVERY SUNDAY and MADE ON BROADWAY.

Now she found herself paired for the first time with her studio buddy, Mickey Rooney, in a routine program picture called THOROUGHBREDS DON'T CRY.

A TEAM!

Had Mickey and Judy become an off-screen team as well? They had technically barely made puberty—but hothouse babies are quite different.

Did they, or didn't they? Judy says no. Mickey says yes.

Thoroughbreds Don't Cry   *1937*

Babes in Arms   *1939*

Judy once said, "The whole trouble was we met when we were too damned young, so it was all puppy stuff. A few years later, maybe something real could have happened. I was really crazy about that little bastard. Not only him, but his talent, too. Maybe we could have been a real forever team. As it turned out, we seemed to have an Olympic marrying competition. Five for me and seven for him. So far, that is. But he must be slowing down, don't you think so? Who knows, maybe one of these days I'll catch up with him."

The great stroke of luck for the TEAM was MGM's acquisition of the glorious Rodgers and Hart show, BABES IN ARMS.

The TEAM captured the imagination of the public in no uncertain manner and went on soaringly to STRIKE UP THE BAND, LIFE BEGINS FOR ANDY HARDY, BABES ON BROADWAY, GIRL CRAZY, THOUSANDS CHEER, and WORDS AND MUSIC.

Dazzling youth was the order of the day.

Best to leave it there. The future was unkind to Judy Garland. Judy went up and down, and up and down, and out.

No one seems to know or to remember how Joe Yule, Junior, became Mickey Rooney, but the story of Frances Gumm metamorphosing into Judy Garland is well documented. Little Frances Gumm was one-third of the Gumm sisters, the youngest. One of the big moments in their act was Baby (Frances) sitting up on the piano and singing "My Man."

Once at the Oriental Theater in Chicago, the Gumm Sisters appeared as a replacement act. The master of ceremonies was George Jessel. He introduced them. "Ladies and gentlemen, it is my pleasure to present a new act— the Gumm Sisters." The audience laughed. Jessel was known, of course, as a comedian, and anything he said was taken as funny. But it did damage the performance. Even though the team had been working under that name for some time, Jessel thought it no good. He was particularly impressed by the tiny twelve-year-old Frances. Finally, he went to her mother and said, "Mrs. Gumm, the name of your act is ridiculous. If it was a comedy act, it would be different, but it's not. I advise you to change

the name."

"Change it to what?" she asked.

"I don't know. I'll think of something."

Before going on to introduce them for the second show, he said to the girls, "You got a new name."

"What is it?" they asked.

"You'll see," he said.

He went out on the stage, and after his monologue, said, "Ladies and gentlemen, it is my pleasure to present a new act—the Garland Sisters."

Later, Jessel was asked how he had come up with that particular name. He explained that between shows, he had been on the telephone with a friend of his, Robert Garland, the theatre critic of the New York *World-Telegram*. And as he hung up, he thought—"Garland." Yes, that would be a nice name for those kids.

Thus Frances Gumm became Frances Garland. The Judy part came later. Hoagy Carmichael had written a daringly audacious song called "Judy," the last lines of which ran:

> "If you think she's a saint
> And you find that she ain't
> That's Judy. . . ."

Something about the name appealed to Frances. It seemed sexy and faintly wicked. She appropriated it for herself. She dropped Frances and said to her sisters, "And I don't ever want to hear 'Baby' again, either." Thus Judy Garland.

Under the relentless prodding and promotion of a terrifying stage mother, Ethel Gumm, Judy moved into the mainstream of the talents of her time.

According to California law, children of school age must be provided with an education. Consequently, MGM had a school for all their underage players.

The scenery department had created it. A one-story wooden schoolhouse, painted red, with a little front porch. It was indeed a little red schoolhouse.

When things went wrong at Metro, and, in an economy wave, it was abandoned and the kids sent out to public schools, Harry Kurnitz referred to the building as "the little in-the-red schoolhouse."

The teacher at the school was Miss Mary MacDonald, who was extremely popular with her pupils.

It was here that Mickey Rooney and Judy Garland met. They seemed to be a TEAM almost at once, made for each other. She laughed at his jokes, he paid her callow compliments by the barrel.

Judy Garland suffered from scoliosis—a minor spine curvature. It was entirely hereditary. Her grandmother had had it, and her mother before her. Both her daughters suffer from it in a minor degree. It gives the impression of a slight humpback and prevents the growth of a long neck.

L. B. Mayer would sometimes greet her jokingly, saying, "And how's my little hunchback today?" Dainty L. B. At other times, he would use the description in a less affectionate key: "Get that goddamned little hunchback up here. I'll straighten her out."

In either case, not precisely the sort of comment to instill confidence.

Through Mickey, Judy was soon part of the young film community, which included Deanna Durbin, Peggy Ryan, Freddie Bartholomew, Donald O'Connor, and others.

The sister act was finished. It was now only Judy who was being primed. Her first picture was a dog called EVERY SUNDAY, in which she was asked to play a ridiculous hillbilly role.

Then nothing much except for a few musical shorts until a spot was found for her in the revue, BROADWAY MELODY OF 1938. She sang "Dear Mr. Gable" and electrified audiences.

And it was on this picture, at the age of fifteen, that she began to take Benzedrine, then Dexedrine and Dexamyl, and stayed hooked on drugs of one kind or another for the rest of her life.

Following BROADWAY MELODY OF 1938, the Mickey Rooney–Judy Garland TEAM was born, although no one at the studio was aware of it. She was cast in a Mickey Rooney picture called THOROUGHBREDS DON'T CRY, and played Sophie Tucker's niece. Sophie ran a boarding house, and Mickey played a young jockey.

From the first, Mickey Rooney assumed an avuncular attitude toward Judy, coaching her, helping her, directing her, sometimes imitating her. He called her "Joots," and when asked why, he replied simply, "It's quicker."

Mickey was so smitten with his girlfriend that he insisted on her being given a part in his interminable series of Andy Hardy pictures. This one was called LOVE FINDS ANDY HARDY.

In a magazine article Judy Garland wrote in 1964, she described working with Mickey Rooney on BABES IN ARMS in 1939:

"They'd give us pep-up pills to keep us on our feet long after we were exhausted. Then they'd take us to the studio hospital and knock us cold with sleeping pills—Mickey sprawled on one bed, and me on another. Then, after four hours, they'd wake us up and give us the pep pills again, so we could work another seventy-two hours in a row."

The story is probably apocryphal. It is to be doubted that the Screen Actors Guild would have permitted such scheduling. But there is no doubt that the kids were overworked and exploited.

In dealing with Judy, it sometimes seems as though she were not a young woman with a remarkable voice, but rather a remarkable voice surrounded by a complicated woman.

The voice was one of those freakish accidents, a *lusus naturae*. Even Roger Edens, the most gifted vocal coach in America, was stunned by it. He described it as: "the perfect anatomy for a singer, built around a super muscle of a diaphragm."

Judy's whole life can be measured by the condition of her voice, which again leads one to think of her in terms of a voice first and a person second. When her voice was in shape, she could thrill audiences, choose engagements, be a star. As the voice faded, her hold on the audience came to depend more and more upon pathos, even bathos, sentimentality, nostalgia, and pity, and her powers declined.

Some years ago, I spent a year directing at the Metropolitan Opera House. During my first month there, an old Metropolitan warhorse named Désiré Defrère, who had been a

Babes in Arms *1939*

Strike Up the Band *1940*

Babes in Arms *1939*

Strike Up the Band *1940*

director but was now a backstage official who arranged the curtain calls, invited me to lunch.

"You pitty good," he said, "but I help you."

"Thank you," I said.

"You no trit these singers right. Not right."

"Why not?" I asked.

"You trit like people."

"What about it?"

"Ah hah," he shouted in triumph, "singers they no people. You listen to me, I know. I work all my life with singers. Singers no people."

"What are they?"

"They fricks," he said. *"Fricks!"*

Fricks, I thought. What on earth is he talking about? Fricks? The Frick Collection. Then it hit me. "Freaks" is what he was saying. He went on:

"Inside the troat, inside the chest, the belly, da balls if a man, da monkey business if a lady, is something. I don't know what. *You* don't know what. *They* don't know what. Only God, he knows. He puts it there. Is the voice. Caruso, Chaliapin, Galli-Curci, anybody. What do they know? They gotta voice, that's all. Is like somebody got six fingers. That's all. Great voice don't mean great man or great lady. Don't mean smart. Don't mean intelligent. Don't mean nice. Just means voice. So dey not people, dey *fricks*. You can't act with them, work with them like they real people. You got to work with them like fricks."

As the months went by, I fought this unsavory idea, not always with success. There was something, it turned out, in what Desiré said.

So it was with poor Judy Garland. So it is with many of the current fricks.

As has been seen, some TEAMS spring double Jovelike into being at once, while others take time to develop.

Even though Judy Garland and Mickey Rooney played the principal scenes in LOVE FINDS ANDY HARDY, no one appeared to have perceived them as a TEAM.

Judy was generally well reviewed in the picture. *Variety* said: "Based on her showing,

they will have to find a permanent place for **Miss Garland** in future Hardys." One paper suggested that Judy practically stole the picture. And Archer Winsten of the New York *Post* said: "And, quite surprisingly, Judy Garland is held in such check that one can see great possibilities if she's ever given a chance at a role as far removed as possible from her hot singing characterizations."

BABES IN ARMS came up just in time.

It is a continuing tribute to the wondrous gifts of these two young people that the picture succeeded. In true MGM thirties form, having bought a successful Broadway musical, they proceeded to wreck it, to throw away most of the book, and indeed a good part of the fabulous score.

Anything and everything was tossed in to get a laugh, to get a hand. Almost unbelievably, there was a great-opera-versus-jazz number, and interpolations of songs like "I Cried for You," "Oh, Susanna," "Ida," "By the Light of the Silvery Moon," "I'm Just Wild about Harry," and a rabble-rousing "God's Country."

MGM had still to learn that six composers are not necessarily better than one composer.

When BABES IN ARMS was ready for release, it was decided that, to launch the picture, Mickey Rooney and Judy Garland should accompany it and make a personal appearance, playing four shows a day, perhaps five on weekends, at the Capitol Theatre. Think of it. Mickey Rooney and Judy Garland in BABES IN ARMS, the great Rodgers and Hart Broadway success, and on the stage, Mickey Rooney and Judy Garland *in person!*

"If that doesn't break every record ever for the Capitol, I'll eat their billing," said Howard Strickling, the master publicist of the studio. It was arranged. Endless hoopla and excitement. Finally, there it was, with queues going round and round the block. The show opened.

It broke every existing record for the Capitol, all right, but not in the way that had been anticipated. The first two days recorded among the lowest grosses the Capitol had ever known. Consternation. How could that possibly be? What had happened?

The astonishing thing is that no one connected with the theatre or with the studio had foreseen the impending situation. What had happened was simply this: The first audience came in, and having seen the picture and the stage show, decided to see the picture and stage show again. Some stayed all day, seeing all four shows, and subsisting on chocolate bars and popcorn or the lunches they had brought in their own brown bags. Thus the turnover did not amount to grosses for five complete shows, but more like two shows. It was too late to change the policy of the theatre, although later in the engagement, it was attempted. Many ticket buyers claimed it was a violation of their rights. There were demonstrations, near riots, but somehow the theatre managed to achieve a kind of policing and insisted upon clearing the theatre at the end of every performance.

The venture succeeded largely because the audience sensed the birth of a TEAM. By this time, the studio did, as well. Another Andy Hardy was planned with Judy playing the same part (Betsy Booth) she had played in the earlier Hardy picture.

The success of BABES IN ARMS gave the studio courage to repeat its mistakes with STRIKE UP THE BAND. This had been a brilliant Broadway musical with a book by George S. Kaufman and Morrie Ryskind and a score by the Gershwins. Again, most of the book and score was scrapped and an MGM musical created. No matter. Rooney and Garland carried it. Even though the *New York Times* complained a bit: "As they say in Hollywood, this show has everything—music, laughter, tears. . . . As usual, everything is a little too much."

The TEAM was working well and would have worked even better had Judy Garland been able to discipline herself and work in a more professional way. As it was, she leaned heavily on her instinctive facility, rehearsed only when forced to, and performed often in a largely improvisational manner.

Few Metro contract players were able to get away with this sort of behavior, not even Clark Gable or Spencer Tracy or Jean Harlow or William Powell or Myrna Loy. But Judy Garland did. The reasons for this were gos-

Babes on Broadway *1942*

Girl Crazy *1943*

Girl Crazy *1943*

Babes on Broadway *1942*

Words and Music *1948*

siped about, eyebrows bounced, fans were whispered behind, tidbits dropped through the nose or clenched teeth or the side of the mouth. Judy seemed to have the studio buffaloed.

Rooney was later quoted as saying: "Judy has the uncanny ability to get in there and pull it off. When we made BABES IN ARMS and STRIKE UP THE BAND, she winged some of the numbers without a hell of a lot of rehearsals, and they worked out just fine. It's this spontaneous thing she has that makes her unique."

Apparently, Rooney was right on because reviewing STRIKE UP THE BAND, *Variety* said: "Miss Garland catches major attention for her all-around achievements. She's right there with Rooney and much of the story as his mentoring girlfriend, teams with him in the production numbers for both songs and dances and rings the bell with several songs sold to the utmost."

There you have it again. What matters is not the method, but the result.

The TEAM was in high now, and there was a real demand from audiences to see Rooney and Garland together as much as possible. Invention apparently flagged because we were back with Andy Hardy again, and Judy played her Betsy Booth part for the third time.

With great care, a romantic consummation was avoided. Doubtless the front office was dreaming of still another pairing in another Andy Hardy movie, but thank Fortune, it was never to be.

Instead, a sequel manqué to BABES IN ARMS was planned, to be called BABES ON BROADWAY.

In this one, in addition to the prepared numbers, Rooney and Garland walk into an empty old theatre and suddenly do imaginative impressions of great figures of the past. So there we see Rooney doing scenes from CYRANO DE BERGERAC (!) in the manner of Richard Mansfield, then all at once he is Harry Lauder, singing "I Belong to Glasgow." Garland becomes Fay Templeton, and as if that were not enough, she is Blanche Ring singing "Rings on My Fingers," and becomes Sarah Bernhardt—you heard me—singing "La Marseillaise."

Had enough? Wait. Here comes Rooney as Carmen Miranda, and sings "Mama Yo Quiero" in Spanish.

Another one of their pictures, THOUSANDS CHEER, had absolutely nothing to do with the Irving Berlin–Moss Hart masterpiece, AS THOUSANDS CHEER. It was simply a wartime paste-up job, and careful observers of the film scene were beginning to suspect that MGM was using Rooney and Garland carelessly, holding nothing back, allowing them to let go without form or discipline on too many occasions, and using their talents in a profligate way.

A surfeit of anything is unhealthy. Certainly it is possible to have too much talent. Talent is a responsibility. Great talent is a burden.

It is in this connection that one must view the dismal saga of Judy Garland and the bleak story of Mickey Rooney.

But whatever happened to them as time took its toll, as a TEAM they were a dream. Young, vivacious, filled with aspiration and hope, and there before us, opening a magic box filled with unbelievable and constantly surprising tricks. They could sing and dance and act serious scenes and be excruciatingly funny. They could behave like grown-ups in all their complexities. They had a deep and abiding appreciation of each other personally and professionally, and it showed in every frame of film they did.

In the spring of 1940, the Academy of Motion Picture Arts and Sciences created a special "juvenile" Academy Award for the Best Juvenile Performance of the Year. It was given to Judy Garland for THE WIZARD OF OZ. The sentimental presenter on that occasion was Mickey Rooney.

Toward the end of her life, when Judy was in every kind of trouble there is—physical, mental, domestic, financial—she was a patient at the Peter Bent Brigham Hospital in Boston. Mickey, loyal to the end, phoned her con-

stantly, attempting to stimulate her ambition and renew her confidence in herself.

In June 1963, at the end of one of the worst years of Judy's life, she put together a television series for CBS. Her old friend and collaborator, Mort Lindsey, was engaged as musical director. Mel Tormé was writing special material. George Schlatter, one of the best television producers, was in charge. And who would be the best guest star for her first show? Mickey Rooney, of course.

On the opening show, Mickey departed from the script to put his arm about Judy, look into the camera, and say to the television audience: "This is the love of my life. There isn't an adjective in the world to express my love for Judy. She's Judy, and that's all there is to say."

He and Judy worked, they practiced, they helped one another, they drilled, they sweated as of old. But will was no substitute for passion. The series struggled along for a time and failed.

About their partnership, Mickey Rooney once said, "We were the space people of our day. We just had to look at one another and we'd crack up—each one knew instantly what the other was thinking."

"She shot up like a rocket," wrote one observer, "and came down like a charred stick."

Long after Mickey Rooney and Judy Garland had worked together as a triumphant TEAM, he stayed close to her, keeping the TEAM alive. In 1965, Judy was to play a six-night engagement at the Greek Theater in Los Angeles. Just before it, she tripped over her dog (she said) and broke her left elbow. She went on and tried to perform with her arm in a cast. It was something less than joyous for the audience, when all at once, down the aisle came the irrepressible Mickey. He jumped onto the stage and did the show with her—gratis, of course.

Judy, in the fashion of the day, used a hand mike, although God knows she didn't need it. With her arm in a cast, handling the mike was difficult, if not impossible. Mickey held the mike for her.

DREAM TEAMS

Robert De Niro and Clara Bow

Greta Garbo and Humphrey Bogart

Rudolph Valentino and Faye Dunaway

Jean Harlow and Marlon Brando

Without Love *1945*

Without Love *1945*

Sea of Grass *1947*

A Perfect Pair
SPENCER TRACY and KATHARINE HEPBURN

My own personal favorite TEAM of all is, of course, Spencer Tracy and Katharine Hepburn. I am not in the least prejudiced by the fact that I had a hand in the formation of this TEAM. After all these years, I can view it quite objectively, and it seems to me that more than any two screen partners I have ever seen, Tracy and Hepburn are the best.

Their interplay and action and reaction, talking and listening, sense of spontaneity, invention, are all of the highest order.

In my judgment, Spencer Tracy is the finest American film actor ever. This view is shared by virtually every other film actor I have ever known.

Spencer's work underlines the wisdom of less is more. By the end of his career, he had virtually eliminated "acting" from his work and substituted "being." To understand fully the depth of this achievement, one has only to try to think of who else on the screen has ever done it or is doing it.

Spencer Tracy was born in Milwaukee, Wisconsin, on April 5, 1900. Following a rigorous Catholic education, he seriously considered the priesthood as a life work until his closest pal, Pat O'Brien, announced *his* determination to go to New York and become an actor. Spencer went with him. They soon learned that the opportunities for completely untrained tyros were rare, and so together they enrolled in the American Academy of Dramatic Arts.

Upon graduation, they shared not only a one-room apartment, but one good suit, which would be worn by the one who had an interview, an audition, or a reading.

One must remember that at this time—the early twenties—most young actors were handsome. Both Spencer and Pat were certainly not actory. Still they each managed to find work in stock companies around the country. Spencer moving from Baltimore, Maryland, to Providence, Rhode Island, to Grand Rapids, Michigan, learning his trade, developing a personality. At length, New York and a small part in A ROYAL FANDANGO with Ethel Barrymore. Not long after, an engagement with his idol, George M. Cohan.

Rehearsing with Cohan, he recalled, was a heady experience. He was virtually immobilized with tension. He remembers a fateful moment during the fifth day of rehearsal when he saw Cohan come slowly down the aisle. He knew that he was moments from being dismissed. Cohan reached the apron of the stage and looked up at Spencer, who by now was prepared for the worst.

"Young man," said Cohan, "you're the best actor I ever saw."

Spencer Tracy's career was well and truly launched.

In 1930, his part turned up—Killer Mears in THE LAST MILE, by John Wexley. His electrifying performance in this overwhelming play, directed by Chester Erskine, established him as a star with limitless potential.

It was at this time that John Ford was preparing a prison comedy called UP THE RIVER, and it did not take super imagination for the East Coast scouts to think of Tracy for the role in it.

So began his film career, which he had planned to be brief, but it was seventeen years before he was to return to the theatre.

In those seventeen years, he became one of Hollywood's most spectacular stars. There appeared to be no end to his range and versatility. He played comedies: QUICK MILLIONS, SIX CYLINDER LOVE, ME AND MY GAL, THE SHOW OFF, LIBELED LADY; dramas: 20,000 YEARS IN SING SING, THE POWER AND THE GLORY, MAN'S CASTLE, FURY, SAN FRANCISCO, CAPTAINS COURAGEOUS, BOYS TOWN, DR. JEKYLL AND MR. HYDE; action pictures: SKY DEVILS, DANTE'S INFERNO, TEST PILOT, NORTHWEST PASSAGE; biographical pictures: EDISON THE MAN; mysteries; thrillers; melodramas—excelling in all.

When an actor plays as effortlessly, as casually, as easily as Tracy appears to do, it is sometimes thought that the work comes easily. This was not so in the case of Spencer Tracy, who sweated over every part. He studied and thought and felt and gave himself fully to the material.

He eschewed makeup, believing that it interfered with the purity of expression and, moreover, saw it (perhaps unreasonably) as a kind of crutch.

"If you want to wear a mask," he once thundered, "wear one. Don't paint it on or paste it on or putty it on. A mask is one thing, a face is something else. The old Greeks did it all with masks, but I don't want to."

We were as close as brothers, and thus could engage in quarrels, sometimes bitter, but never permanent. One of them occurred when I was directing him in Robert E. Sherwood's play, THE RUGGED PATH. The play contained a scene in which the character played by Tracy emerges from the sea onto one of the Philippine Islands, having been shipwrecked for five days. I arranged an unshaven beard effect with a brilliant makeup man, Eddie Senz. It was made of a curious combination of stretchable fiber and latex, could be put on and taken off in two seconds, and required no spirit gum, or glue of any kind. When it was demonstrated to Tracy, he simply turned and walked away. I followed him to his dressing room.

"What's the matter?" I asked.

"Nothing. I don't need that."

"Wait a second, Spence."

"Save your breath. I'm not putting anything on my face."

"Spence, be reasonable, willya."

"Why should I?"

"Will you listen a minute?"

"No."

"The guy's been shipwrecked for five days. How can he possibly turn up clean-shaven?"

"Never mind."

"It'll look ridiculous. It'll bother the audience."

"No, it won't."

"Why won't it?"

"Because I'll act unshaven," he said.

It was my turn to give up and walk away.

Unlike members of other TEAMS, Tracy was a great star individually. In 1941, when he and Katharine Hepburn met, he had already made forty-five pictures. He had been nominated for the Academy Award several times and had won it twice: for CAPTAINS COURAGEOUS and for BOYS TOWN.

The MGM roster in those days was dizzyingly powerful and glamorous, but no player on the lot commanded greater esteem—from the rarefied Olympian latitudes of the Front Office to the waiting line of extras at the Washington Boulevard Gate. His teaming with Katharine Hepburn gave the public one of those miraculous gifts that occur rarely.

Katharine Hepburn, too, was and is a superstar. It can be said of her that she has been a film star longer than any player in history. She was a star in her first movie, A BILL OF DIVORCEMENT, in 1932. She is a star in 1981 —nearly fifty years of stardom. One-fourth of that is enough to exhaust most players, but not Katharine Houghton Hepburn, who was born in Hartford, Connecticut, on November 9, 1907 (according to some records; on November 8, 1909, according to others) —one of her many whimsical notions is that she keeps her actual birthday a secret. It is not a question of vanity—she is the least vain actress extant—it is simply that she believes it to be nobody's business. Her father was a distinguished physician; her mother, an early feminist. And Katharine was the maverick in a large and lively family. Growing up, she became a brilliant student and a remarkable athlete. Her unique beauty and bursting vitality (and she knew precisely what to do with her beauty and her vitality) appeared to make her destined for the stage. Following her graduation from Bryn Mawr, she stormed the Broadway gates and began her acting career.

She burst into the Hollywood constellation in the manner of a nova with her first film, A BILL OF DIVORCEMENT, and followed it dazzlingly with MORNING GLORY, CHRISTOPHER STRONG, and LITTLE WOMEN, in hardly more than a single year. Ups and downs had followed, until, panicked by the notorious Box Office Poison advertisement, RKO had settled her contract.

Her Broadway triumph in THE PHILADELPHIA STORY made it possible for her to re-enter films—she had wisely acquired the motion-picture rights—and she was an in-demand star once again.

Still, it was a crucial career moment for

her. Comebacks often fizzle if they are not solidified. Suspense . . .

Then: "Spencer Tracy and Katharine Hepburn in WOMAN OF THE YEAR."

A great new life began. A TEAM had been formed and was to endure, stunningly, for twenty-five years.

What was it that made Tracy and Hepburn so remarkably effective a TEAM?

Even though the idea of the teaming was mine, I cannot answer the question. It was simply (or not so simply) an instinct, a feeling of rightness, a hunch.

Alas, the movies are no less complex than life itself, and solutions are complex. Answers are easier than questions.

It has been suggested that the Tracy-Hepburn magic was occasioned by contrast. He, a rough realist; she, a classy, airy sprite. The personalities clash in Reel One, struggle for supremacy in the next eight, seesaw precariously, and finally, happily blend in Reel Ten. Of course. Contrast. High and low. Rich and poor. Low brow and high tone. All right? No.

The contrast notion seems good until one considers other splendid TEAMS. William Powell and Myrna Loy. Irene Dunn and Cary Grant. Nelson Eddy and Jeanette MacDonald. Mickey Rooney and Judy Garland. Contrast?

A superlative TEAM appears to be as hard to achieve as a great marriage. It is, in fact, a marriage of sorts, and requires the same delicate balance.

The partners must attempt to share and exchange respect, admiration, loyalty, unselfishness, understanding, strength, challenge, and humor—each bringing out the best in the other.

Why are there today so few significantly popular TEAMS?

One answer is that the breakdown of the major studio method of production has put an end to planned career continuity.

Throughout the formative years of the Tracy-Hepburn partnership, both were under contract to MGM. Thus, the studio and its creative minds sought out vehicles to fit their stars or TEAMS.

MGM provided SEA OF GRASS, KEEPER OF THE FLAME, STATE OF THE UNION, WITHOUT LOVE.

Woman of the Year *1942*

Woman of the Year *1942*

Woman of the Year *1942*

Woman of the Year *1942*

Woman of the Year *1942*

91

State of the Union *1948*

Desk Set *1957*

Keeper of the Flame *1943*

Without Love *1945*

Desk Set *1957*

Adam's Rib *1949*

Guess Who's Coming to Dinner   *1967*

Sea of Grass   *1947*

Guess Who's Coming to Dinner   *1967*

Guess Who's Coming to Dinner   *1967*

Without Love   *1945*

On the set of Guess Who's Coming to Dinner

Ruth Gordon and I created ADAM'S RIB and PAT AND MIKE especially for them.

Twentieth Century-Fox offered them THE DESK SET when their Metro contracts expired, and it is a fair guess that William Rose and Stanley Kramer had them in mind from the beginning for GUESS WHO'S COMING TO DINNER.

Can it be that the free-wheeling system of present-day production cannot afford the luxury of TEAM planning?

Another, deeper reason has been suggested: that the highly competitive, razor-sharp rivalry of independent production has developed too many stars who are incapable (or at least, un-desirous) of spotlight sharing. I wonder.

In any case, those of us who knew the great TEAMS, admired them and enjoyed them, miss them. We looked forward to each new venture; we watched the pairs grow together.

Compare the Tracy-Hepburn teamwork in their last film, GUESS WHO'S COMING TO DIN-NER. with that in their first—WOMAN OF THE YEAR. Rich and vibrant though it was in the beginning, the ripening years brought it to a rare perfection. The kind of acting they did together is not achieved swiftly or easily. Lunt and Fontanne were not built in a day.

I maintain that the ability to work as part of a TEAM is one of the noblest of human achievements.

Strange. Spencer Tracy, who possessed this ability in boundless measure, did not agree with me. It caused, in fact, one of our long-continuing debates, resulting (as do most de-bates) in each one's clinging even more firmly to his own precept.

Spencer was an original, a unique man who believed firmly in the glory of the individual. One of his abiding heroes was Henry David Thoreau, whose work he knew fully and inti-mately. Thoreau's Walden days especially fas-cinated Spencer.

I argued that learning to live alone (whether in Walden or Beverly Hills) was not the answer to the human predicament; that this was the wrong end of the stick; that learn-ing to live together was the basic responsibil-ity—particularly in these days of population explosion, with more and more of us rubbing up against one another in so many new ways.

I never convinced Spencer and thought it odd that he, a shining exemplar of professional teamwork, should continue to stay hipped on the subject of the individual.

Watch him on the screen (especially with Katharine Hepburn) as he listens—really lis-tens, not merely assuming the attitudes of listen-ing. Watch him talk to the others—to them. Watch him react—truly, instinctively. You will see the art of acting and the spirit of teamwork there before your eyes.

We all love to see a TEAM at work—on the stage, on a playing field, in an operating room—because it tells us something about de-pendence and interdependence. It reassures us with intimations of the awesome power of hu-man beings pursuing a common cause. It af-fords us a vision of what is best in life.

On the screen, in my time, no one did it better than Tracy and Hepburn.

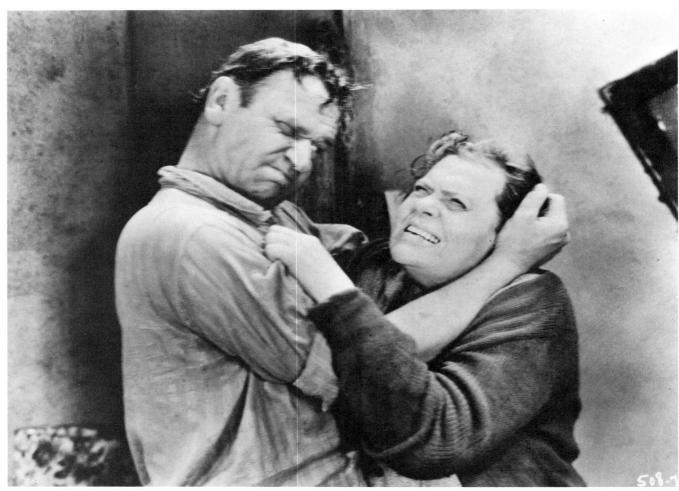

Min and Bill *1930*

Min and Bill   *1930*

Min and Bill
WALLACE BEERY and MARIE DRESSLER

Neither one of them was a likely movie star. A supporting player, yes. Characters, comedy relief, truckdriver, prison warden, funny schoolteacher, yes; but superstar? Unlikely. And yet it happened for them singly and in tandem.

Marie Dressler's real name was Leila von Koerber. She was born in 1869 and lived several lives. Her theatrical background was complete: opera, burlesque, vaudeville, theatre. Following her Broadway and road hit (a five-year run), TILLIE'S NIGHTMARE, she was signed by Mack Sennett. The year was 1914. Marie was forty-four, making her screen debut.

Mack Sennett, dubbed "Father Goose" by Gene Fowler, controlled a considerable stable of comedians at the time. His eye was ever out for new talent and his memory, as well, as witness this telegram sent to a young comedian playing in Philadelphia in 1912 in an act called A NIGHT IN AN ENGLISH MUSIC HALL.

CHARLES CHAPLIN
BROAD STREET THEATRE
PHILADELPHIA, PENN.
ARE YOU THE MAN WHO PLAYED THE
DRUNK IN THE BOX IN THE ORPHEUM
THEATRE THREE YEARS AGO STOP IF SO
WILL YOU GET IN TOUCH WITH KESSEL
AND BAUMANN LONGACRE THEATRE
N.Y.
MACK SENNETT

Chaplin's recalled version of this historic telegram is that it was sent to the troupe's manager, Reeves, and read:

IS THERE A MAN NAMED CHAFFIN IN
YOUR COMPANY OR SOMETHING LIKE
THAT STOP IF SO WILL HE COMMUNI-
CATE WITH KESSEL AND BAUMANN 24
LONGACRE BUILDING BROADWAY
MACK SENNETT

Chaplin did as instructed with some misgivings—but when Kessel and Baumann, the owners of Keystone, offered him $150 a week for a tryout year, he accepted. Among Sennett's players were Roscoe Arbuckle, Ford Sterling, and the incomparable Mabel Normand.

Chaplin's career with Sennett began badly. His first short, MAKING A LIVING, was a dud. He was next teamed with Mabel Normand in MABEL'S STRANGE PREDICAMENT, with somewhat better results, but still not satisfactory from Sennett's point of view. Mack Sennett, the master of silent-screen comedy, did not think that Charlie Chaplin was funny. It may have been the ocean between that caused this blind spot. British humor and American has always been different. As George Bernard Shaw said, "England and America are two countries divided by a common language."

Sennett now believed he had made a mistake and tried to settle Chaplin's contract. Chaplin turned him down—$150 a week for a year was a dream come true and he was not prepared to give it up. Besides he *did* think he was funny.

"What did you feel," I once asked him, "when George Jean Nathan and Gilbert Seldes and Robert E. Sherwood and the whole literary intelligentsia discovered you and hailed your work as art?"

"Why, nothing," he replied. "Nothing at all. I always knew I was a poet!"

But poets were not in Sennett's line and he did not believe that Chaplin was going to make it. However, since he was paying him, he had to use him, so he put him into the important Marie Dressler picture he was making—TILLIE'S PUNCTURED ROMANCE. In fact, he put just about everyone he owned into it. After all, it was going to be a six-reel picture! So, in addition to Marie Dressler . . . Tillie, the Farmer's Daughter . . . he had

Charlie Chaplin .. The City Slicker
Mabel Normand .... The City Girlfriend
Mack Swain .... Tillie's Father
Edgar Kennedy ...... Cafe Owner
Minta Durfee .... Film Actress
Charles Murray ...... Detective
Charlie Chase .... Detective
Harry McCoy .... Society Guest
Chester Conklin .... Society Guest

An all-star cast in fact, not merely in billing.

TILLIE'S PUNCTURED ROMANCE exceeded even Mack Sennett's expectations and as the record-breaking grosses rolled in, he began to

Min and Bill *1930*

Min and Bill *1930*

think that Charlie Chaplin *was* funny.

Charlie and Marie wooing by throwing bricks at each other. Charlie jumping on Marie's back and riding her like a horse—nothing was going to prevent the City Slicker's pursuit of the Farmer's Daughter. Today, sixty-four years after it was made, it is still shown.

Strangely, parts for Marie Dressler did not materialize, and after a few lean years, she returned to the legitimate theatre, where she fared not much better. In the twenties, she could be seen by passersby sitting at her desk in the real-estate office on Madison Avenue in New York City where she was employed.

Ten years later, when the movies began to talk and experienced stage players were at a premium, someone remembered Marie Dressler, and she returned to Hollywood to make THE CALLAHANS AND THE MURPHYS, THE JOY GIRL, BREAKFAST AT SUNRISE, BRINGING UP FATHER, THE PATSY, THE DIVINE LADY, THE HOLLYWOOD REVUE, THE VAGABOND LOVER, and CHASING RAINBOWS.

And then—as Marthy with Greta Garbo in ANNA CHRISTIE, she exploded as a full-fledged star, made a number of successful films and was teamed in the first of a splendid series with Polly Moran—CAUGHT SHORT, REDUCING, POLITICS, and PROSPERITY.

In 1930, a story caused the formation of a TEAM that captured the imagination of the public at once. It had warmth and humanity and humor, audacity and vigor and profundity: MIN AND BILL. The story was, as they say, a "natural," especially when class material for Beery and Dressler was hard to come by.

Wallace Beery was born in Kansas City, Missouri, in 1889. It tells a good deal about him that he regularly informed interviewers that he spent three years in the fourth grade. He used to tell how he was two heads taller than the tallest of his classmates who called him "Jumbo."

"I was famous for two things," he recalls. "Dumbness and awkwardness."

His father was a Kansas City cop, who must have been embarrassed when his son first appeared on the stage as a chorus boy and then made his movie debut as a female impersonator.

But in 1907, when he was twenty-one, he was a musical-comedy star of sorts with his name in lights on Broadway. His show-business career had begun when he was sixteen and he joined the famous Forepaugh-Sells Circus as an elephant man.

Later, his brother Noah got him a job in the chorus of BABES IN TOYLAND. This led to jobs in THE PRINCE OF PILSEN, THE STUDENT KING, THE YANKEE TOURIST, and a JAPANESE NIGHTINGALE. In this last, he finally got to speak lines—two.

In THE YANKEE TOURIST, he was understudy to the star, Raymond Hitchcock, and those who remember Hitchcock say that if you never saw him, never mind—just look at Wallace Beery and you will. This may be going a bit far, but Beery always acknowledged his debt to Hitchy, in the same way that Spencer Tracy felt that *his* principal influence had been George M. Cohan.

Shortly after Wallace Beery entered films (playing a Swedish maid for Essanay) he met and married a young starlet named Gloria Swanson. The marriage did not survive, but they remained friends across the years.

"I was too young for her," he once explained.

The Beery-Dressler teaming was an inspiration. They brought out not only the best in each other, but the funniest. A tough TEAM to analyze—who is playing straight? Who is the comic? Which one male? Which female? They complemented one another beautifully.

MIN AND BILL was a triumph, and the search for material was on.

TUGBOAT ANNIE was found but Beery raised hell. The title, leaving him out, seemed to relegate him to a supporting role although the part was every bit as good as hers.

Robert Hopkins (Hoppy), the renowned MGM wag, attempted to placate him.

"What the hell're you talking about, Wally? *You're* in the title."

"I am not."

"You are, too!"

"Where?"

"You've even got top billing."

"How?"

"You play Tugboat and she plays Annie."

"I do not," said Wally.

Title changes were discussed, promised, then forgotten.

Tugboat Annie *1933*

Tugboat Annie *1933*

The truth is that Wally Beery was always the least popular star on the lot. He was stubborn and stolid and generally uncooperative.

Stories of his stinginess were legion. It is said that when one of his closest friends—his press agent, Bill Newberry—was injured in the Long Beach earthquake and had to spend some months in the hospital, Beery visited him every day and brought a gift-wrapped box containing leftover lunch and dinner delicacies.

He would not—perhaps *could* not—learn lines, making him the bête noire of screenwriters.

Whenever Spencer Tracy became nervous or irritable or testy—his dresser would softly say, "Okay, Wally." Spencer's mock fury would then loosen things up.

TUGBOAT ANNIE topped the success of MIN AND BILL. Metro had, apparently, a new goldmine TEAM.

Beery brought vast experience to the partnership: From his days of farce in silent shorts, through his heavies (German submarine commanders were a specialty), into his association with Doug Fairbanks where he played Richard the Lion-Hearted in ROBIN HOOD, then his teaming with Raymond Hatton for a series of rollicking comedies, followed by a personal success as Butch in the prison epic, THE BIG HOUSE. Other films were FLESH (a western), O'SHAUNESSY'S BOY (an animal trainer), THE CHAMP (a prizefighter), TREASURE ISLAND (Long John Silver). One

gathers that Wallace Beery was a seasoned player.

And Marie Dressler contributed her polished background: Maggie in BRINGING UP FATHER, LET US BE GAY—and her days in the real-estate office.

But poor Marie fell ill and died, unexpectedly. The many projects in work for the TEAM were abandoned.

No one on earth is indispensable. Any one of one hundred now living might disappear overnight, but life and the world would go on. There are, however, those who are irreplaceable, and Marie Dressler was one of these. Unique. Singular. A nonesuch. With her, Wally Beery had met his match; without her, it was all over.

How is it that only two films should convey the idea that they made an extensive series? The answer? Size. Power. Those two films contained enough talent, invention, personality, and fireworks of exchange for a dozen films.

Larger than life people such as Wallace Beery and Marie Dressler are often remembered not only for what they did but for what they might have done.

The Cocoanuts *1929*

The Hilarious Relatives
THE MARX BROTHERS

Once there were five. Julius, Adolph, Leo, Milton, and Herbert.

Later, as a lark, they became Groucho, Harpo, Chico, Gummo, and Zeppo.

How and why and when this transformation? Who knows? The accounts are varied and apocryphal. I have heard seven or eight—two from Groucho, one each from Harpo and Chico, and the rest from Godknows.

One version is that at a time when many novelty acts in vaudeville were taking names such as Bozo, Whango, and Zippo, the Marx boys began to refer to Adolph as "Harpo"—because he played the harp.

(He was self-taught. By the time he learned that he was playing the harp from the wrong side, it was too late to change. He played the harp backward all his life. In later affluent years, he decided to take lessons to improve his technique, and went to Mildred Dilling for lessons. She recounts that the sessions ended with Harpo showing her how he achieved some of his more spectacular effects.)

Julius soon became "Groucho"—a comment on his testy disposition that was to plague him for a lifetime.

Leo was—in the parlance of the day—a skirt-chaser, a chick fancier, so he was "Chicko" until a typo made him "Chico."

Milton was nicknamed "Gummo" because of his affinity for the gum-soled shoes he wore to relieve his bad feet.

No one remembers why Herbert turned into "Zeppo." Perhaps he simply liked the sound. After some years, he tired of being the only straight man in the bunch and left the TEAM to become a fabulously successful agent.

Gummo stayed out of show business for a long time, then he too went into the agency business.

One dates oneself by referring either to the Four Marx Brothers or the Three Marx Brothers or simply the Marx Brothers.

George Bernard Shaw once said: "Cedric Hardwick is my fifth favorite actor, the first four being the Marx Brothers."

They were never not in show business.

Monkey Business   *1931*

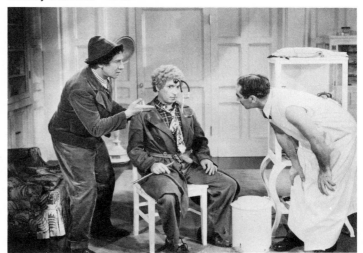

A Day at the Races   *1937*

Monkey Business   *1931*

Horse Feathers *1932*

Room Service *1938*

The Cocoanuts *1929*

The Cocoanuts *1929*

Room Service *1938*

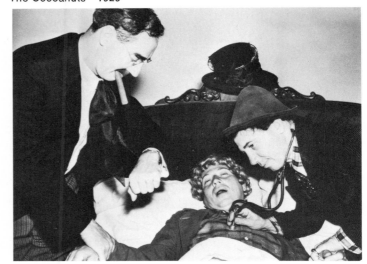
Room Service *1938*

A Night at the Opera   1935

The Cocoanuts   1929

Publicity shot

A Night at the Opera   *1935*

Room Service   *1938*

Room Service   *1938*

A Day at the Races   *1937*

Publicity shot

Duck Soup   *1933*

A Day at the Races   *1937*

Their sainted mother, Minnie, was the sister of Al Shean, of Gallagher and Shean, a famous headline act. "Minnie's boys," as they were known, went on the stage as soon as they could legally escape from school.

First it was Julius, Adolph, and Milton—later joined by Leo. The Four Marx Brothers. Milton is drafted in World War I and is replaced by the youngest brother—Herbert. Still four.

In 1919, the Marx Brothers tried out a book show: THE CINDERELLA GIRL, by Jo Swerling and Gus Kahn. It had a short run in Battle Creek, Michigan, and closed.

With I'LL SAY SHE IS, they made it to Broadway. Then THE COCOANUTS. Wild. ANIMAL CRACKERS. Wilder.

At about this time, both the motion picture art and the motion picture industry were exploded by a bomb called "the talkies." Musical entertainment was in sudden demand. After all, the very first of the so-called "talkies" were actually "singies." Martinelli, Jolson, Grace Moore, and others in the celebrated Vitaphone shorts.

The Marx Brothers were the rage of the Broadway musical stage, so what could be more logical than virtually photographing a Broadway hit?

Thus, while they were appearing at the 44th Street Theatre in ANIMAL CRACKERS, they commuted to Astoria and filmed THE COCOANUTS. Back and forth, back and forth, except on matinee days when they filmed only in the morning, and then returned to 44th Street to play two shows.

Groucho once said, "Sometimes I'd get so punchy that I'd find myself spouting the dialogue from *Animal Crackers* in a scene I was doing in *Cocoanuts*, and vice versa."

But from the release of that first movie, the Marx Brothers belonged to the world.

The development of their distinct personalities is a subject for a behavioral psychologist —not for a simple chronicler.

When they were three, they shared the services of a secretary.

"That must be some tough job," I said.

"What's tough?" asked Oscar Levant.

"Every day she gets a book for Harpo, a herring for Groucho, a broad for Chico—and that's it!"

Diverse, indeed. But on the screen—something else again. A perfectly coordinated comic mechanism.

The casual, knockabout, seemingly improvisational style can be deceptive. These men were stylists, perfectionists, workers, worriers. A missed beat could cause sweat, a missed laugh could bring on a stomachache.

Rehearsals were endless, experiments ceaseless, rewrites, changes. Try this. Try that. Try this again. Faster, slower, louder, softer. Scientists, really.

Cinema Journal for Spring 1969 carries an article, "The Seventeen Preliminary Scripts of *A Day at the Races*."

THE COCOANUTS and ANIMAL CRACKERS were made in the East—at the Paramount Studios on Long Island. With MONKEY BUSINESS, the TEAM moved to Hollywood and took up residence there for good.

HORSE FEATHERS followed. They were piling strength upon strength.

DUCK SOUP was the best yet, followed by A NIGHT AT THE OPERA.

A DAY AT THE RACES began to show the strain of being funny on schedule and to order, and ROOM SERVICE was a mistake.

With THE MARX BROTHERS AT THE CIRCUS, it was clear that invention and inspiration were beginning to flag.

GO WEST was their first failure.

THE BIG STORE heralded the end of it all. No class.

Chico died. But Harpo and Groucho—the survivors—went on to A NIGHT IN CASABLANCA. Not bad, but not a Marx Brothers' picture.

Last of all—desperation. LOVE HAPPY. Story by Harpo Marx. Screenplay by a Hollywood slew—credited and un.

One of the world's most generous traits is that it judges artists by their best—not their worst.

At their best, the Marx Brothers have no equal—their films will be seen and laughed at forever. At their worst, they prove only that they are human, and this is reassuring to those of us who think of them as gods.

Happy Days *1930*

From Seventh Heaven
JANET GAYNOR and CHARLES FARRELL

In Palm Springs, California, a tall, handsome, dignified old gentleman can often be seen walking about the town as if he owned it. He damn near does. A few years ago, he sold the Racquet Club, which he had founded and operated for two decades, in a transaction involving millions. He served as mayor of Palm Springs for seven years, and could be elected again tomorrow if he chose to run. He is outgoing, friendly, and relaxed—the very model of a happy man.

In New York City not long ago, an exhibition of extraordinary flower paintings was shown. It sold out in the first two days. The artist, a tiny, white-haired lady with merry, glistening brown eyes, was often present, accepting praise graciously and filling the gallery from time to time with peals of musical laughter.

Long ago, the old gentleman and the tiny lady comprised the most successful romantic movie TEAM of the day—Janet Gaynor and Charles Farrell.

Her film career began while she was still in her teens, and by 1927, when she was twenty-one, she had already made six movies.

It was with the great silent, SUNRISE, however, directed by F. W. Murnau, that she was established as a major star.

One of the prizes of this success was the part of Diane in the Fox Film Corporation's production of SEVENTH HEAVEN. This was to be the screen version of the Broadway super-smash of the 1922 season, written by Austin Strong and produced by John Golden.

Nothing in show business is surefire, but if anything could be, SEVENTH HEAVEN would be a powerful contender.

It is the story of a simple Parisian sewer laborer (Chico), who befriends an abandoned gamine (Diane) to protect her from the police. He asserts that she is his wife and takes her to his attic dwelling—thus the title SEVENTH HEAVEN. Two nobodies, rejected by society, overlooked by good fortune, create their personal heaven. Then—war. He is gone. He is reported killed. Diane grieves. He returns—blind. No matter. They still have each other and their seventh heaven.

It may sound mawkish, stripped to its bare plot bones, but cast and played truly, it works—and in films, as in the theatre, this is the only measure that matters.

As Janet Gaynor's partner, Fox chose Charles Farrell. Farrell was a strikingly handsome, tall, movie-star-type movie star. He was a Cape Codder, born in Onset, Massachusetts, on August 9, 1902. He began in films in 1923 as an extra, and remained an extra for over a year. His family, believing that he had got this screen-struck madness out of his system at last, urged him to give it up and return to Massachusetts, the real world, and his career in business administration, for which he had been trained. He hesitated. Finally they wired him the money for his return train fare. Facing the facts, he made ready to leave. At the last moment, he was offered a part in WINGS OF YOUTH at Fox. He went on to THE LOVE HOUR and then had the honor of supporting Rin Tin Tin in CLASH OF THE WOLVES. Then a bleak period. In desperation, he accepted a role in a Mack Sennett movie called THE GOSH DARN MORTGAGE, in which he made bad. Back to Fox for SANDY, and A TRIP

TO CHINATOWN. He was then lent out to Paramount for OLD IRONSIDES, directed by James Cruze, and THE ROUGH RIDERS, directed by Victor Fleming.

At Fox, SUNRISE was being prepared by the illustrious F. W. Murnau, and studio gossip had it that Farrell would be costarred in it opposite Lois Moran. But Winfield Sheehan, who was then in charge of production, considered Janet Gaynor his personal protégée, and sold her to Murnau. He was not, however, able to sell him Farrell. The part went to the handsome, manly, wooden George O'Brien. What great difference Murnau saw between these two conventional movie leading men is a mystery he took with him. Perhaps O'Brien's edge was the fact that he was the son of the chief of police of San Francisco.

Janet Gaynor was born Laura Gainor on October 6, 1906, in Philadelphia, Pennsylvania. She moved with her family to Chicago, then Florida, San Francisco, where she was graduated from the Polytechnic High School a few years after George O'Brien, and finally to Los Angeles. By this time, she had acquired an imaginative and ambitious stepfather, Harry C. Jones, known as "Jonesy," who dreamed of getting her into the movies. She had developed into a diminutive, winsome, appealing, vulnerable, virginal type. Thus she possessed in full measure the qualities to which movie audiences of the early twenties responded. They had been brought up on Mary Pickford, and every producer in Hollywood was looking for another Pickford.

After a dreary year working as a bookkeeper in a Los Angeles shoe store and moonlighting as a movie theatre usherette, she decided—with Jonesy's prodding—to become an extra, just like Charlie Farrell, her costar to be.

(Shades of Esther Blodgett, whom she was to portray some fifteen years later. No wonder her attack in the Central Casting scene had such veracity.

"Give it up, honey. Only one in a thousand makes it."

"Well, maybe I'm that one!"

Esther Blodgett was one, and Janet Gaynor was another.)

After four years of extra work, she began to play bits in Hal Roach two-reel comedies. Jonesy was unhappy. He thought she should be a dramatic actress. She went to Universal and played the lead in a two-reel western.

Then—the first important man in her life—Herb Moulton, a newspaperman with connections. He got her a test at Fox, which resulted in the second lead in THE JOHNSTOWN FLOOD, starring George O'Brien and Florence Gilbert. Gaynor scored and was rewarded with a five-year contract at $100 a week. She was given leads in THE SHAMROCK HANDICAP, THE MIDNIGHT KISS, THE BLUE EAGLE (directed by John Ford), and the film version of David Belasco's Broadway success, THE RETURN OF PETER GRIMM. All these in one year. She was now in such great demand that her salary was raised to $300 a week.

Now SUNRISE, a near classic, one of the last great silents. It was at this point that she was teamed with Charles Farrell for SEVENTH HEAVEN.

Delicious   *1931*

The Man Who Came Back   *1931*

Lucky Star   *1929*

The Man Who Came Back   *1931*

The enormous success of this perennial prompted the studio to find "another SEVENTH HEAVEN." STREET ANGEL was the result, a virtual carbon copy. But audiences accepted it.

In 1928, Janet Gaynor won the very first Academy Award. It was given then not for a single picture, but in her case for three: SEVENTH HEAVEN, SUNRISE, and STREET ANGEL.

Jonesy boasted to his pals that little Janet was now making more money than the President of the United States. Winnie Sheehan took personal charge of Janet's career. She was *his* star.

Janet Gaynor recalls: "No one is developing stars the way they were when they put me into *Seventh Heaven*. I remember that I worked as an extra with Clark Gable in a college series. I went to Fox and got these parts, and when he went to Metro, they recognized his potential and he became a star. I give credit to the moguls of those days. They had faith, vision, shrewdness, and they didn't have to go to a committee for a decision."

Sheehan's decision was to put Janet Gaynor into solo starring parts. He gave her CHRISTINA, FOUR DEVILS, but the public made it clear that it wanted to see her with Charles Farrell again. Sheehan obliged with a musical, SUNNY SIDE UP, in which she sang in a small, sweet voice:

"Keep your sunny side up, up
Hide the side that feels blue
If you have nine sons in a row
Baseball teams make money, you know."

After a brief appearance in Fox's all-star revue, HAPPY DAYS, she was teamed once again with Charles Farrell in HIGH SOCIETY BLUES.

A bitter dispute with the studio followed. She felt that she was being destroyed by typecasting and poor pictures. She walked off the lot and left town. The studio punished her with a suspension, and as an additional blow, took her out of LILIOM and gave the costarring role with Charles Farrell to Rose Hobart. As in the case of many suspensions, both sides suffered. Hobart and Farrell were no Gaynor and Farrell, and the picture failed.

Janet Gaynor returned and was given a stark dramatic role—just what she wanted—THE MAN WHO CAME BACK, with Charles Farrell. She played a nightclub star who becomes a dope fiend; Farrell was a blue-blood who turns into an alcoholic.

Janet Gaynor later said, "It was positively the worst picture I ever made."

The public agreed, and she was rushed into DADDY LONG LEGS, opposite Warner Baxter—Charles Farrell having turned down the part as too old. The picture was a smash.

Janet then made TESS OF THE STORM COUNTRY with Farrell (a Mary Pickford remake), but said no vehemently when the studio wanted her to do another Mary Pickford remake, REBECCA OF SUNNYBROOK FARM. Fox put Marian Nixon into it, hoping to build her into a Janet Gaynor replacement. Gaynor was getting too feisty for the studio's slave system. But Nixon was no Gaynor either, and proved it by failing to team successfully with Charles Farrell in two pictures.

Before TESS, Gaynor and Farrell had made three more movies: MERELY MARY ANN, DELICIOUS (with a Gershwin score), and THE FIRST YEAR (from the Broadway hit).

The TEAM was fading. It had used up its bag of tricks.

Janet Gaynor was flourishing on her own in STATE FAIR, with Will Rogers; ADORABLE (another Gershwin score); and PADDY THE NEXT BEST THING, with Warner Baxter.

At this point, 1934, Janet Gaynor was second only to Marie Dressler in the popularity polls for Box-Office Queen.

Next came CAROLINA, after which the studio thought a four-star arrangement might save the TEAM. The film was CHANGE OF HEART, with James Dunn and Ginger Rogers as the second team. In reel one, Gaynor and Dunn, Farrell and Rogers. By reel ten—well—change of heart.

It was the twelfth and last Janet Gaynor–Charles Farrell movie.

Janet, on her own, went up up up. Farrell was less successful, probably because he was getting weary of it all and began to spend more and more time in Palm Springs, finally becoming part of it—commercially, socially, civically. He remained a charming, warm, engaging man.

High Society Blues   *1930*

Street Angel   *1929*

The First Year *1932*

Sunny Side Up *1929*

The First Year *1932*

Sunny Side Up *1929*

Street Angel *1929*

Street Angel *1929*

High Society Blues   *1930*

Lucky Star   *1929*

Merely Mary Ann   *1931*

The Man Who Came Back   *1931*

Merely Mary Ann   *1931*

Delicious   *1931*

He never returned to films, but was the star of one of television's first popular series, MY LITTLE MARGIE. Following its successful run, he did another television show, playing himself as owner and manager of the Racquet Club. This one did less well, and after the death of his wife, Virginia Valli, in 1968, he retired from acting.

No one knows for certain if the TEAM had an off-screen life, as frequently hinted at by the numberless gossip columnists of the day.

Both spend a good deal of time denying it. "There was nothing in the world I wouldn't have done for Charlie," Janet said. "And I know there is nothing in the world he wouldn't have done for me, but it wasn't the marrying kind of love. No one understands. No one believes us. But it's true. . . . If we wanted to marry, there wasn't anything to stop us. We had years alone together with nothing to interfere. As far as personal interest was concerned, it was to our advantage to marry. It would have pleased everyone—the studio, the public. But you can't marry just to please others. . . . I wanted romance—and Charlie never did. That is, not all the time. . . . Anyway, I guess I was too smart to marry an actor. I never have. Actors are terribly attractive, but not to commit your life to."

Eventually, Janet Gaynor married a San Francisco lawyer, Lydell Peck.

"My first marriage was just foolish," she says. "I was young and I just wanted to be married. At that time you didn't go off and live with someone. But the marriage was not right from the beginning."

Later she married the great MGM designer, Adrian, by whom she has a son.

With Adrian she lived on a great, luxurious, sprawling ranch in the Valley. My wife and I visited them there once, and Janet told us excitedly about a recent adventure they had had, a terrible fire in the main house.

"It all happened so suddenly," she said, "in the middle of the night. We knew we had to get out of the house, and so we each grabbed just one thing and ran. We knew we never would be able to get back in again."

"If you don't mind my asking," I said, "what did Adrian take?"

"The safe," she replied. "I mean, everything he could carry out of the safe."

"And you?"

"Why, my stills," she said simply.

After Adrian's death, Janet Gaynor married Paul Gregory, the producer. In one of her rare interviews she was quoted as saying about her retirement from the screen: "I really felt that I had had it all—the cream of life. I had loved the pleasure and excitement of being at the top and I wanted to know about other things in life. I felt I didn't want to spend my whole life being an actress. I spent years never seeing anything because I had to sit with my back to the room in a restaurant, and in the days of the silents, everybody wanted to touch you because they didn't think you were real. . . . But I think I had a wonderful career. I enjoyed it all and have no sad tales to tell you."

The Big Sleep *1946*

Whistle!
HUMPHREY BOGART and LAUREN BACALL

The teaming of Humphrey Bogart and Lauren Bacall had a number of elements that made it extraordinary. To begin with, when they met, he was more than twice her age. Moreover, he was an important star, and she had yet to make her first picture.

Hers was a modern Cinderella story. She was born Betty Ann Perske in Brooklyn, and spent her girlhood dreaming of a stage career. She went to Julia Richman High School, and even there was thought of as the "actressy" one. She was indeed striking and exceptionally photogenic and glamorous.

The jingle in her high school classbook (June 1940) reads:

"Popular ways that win.
May your dream of an actress
overflow the brim."

She had taken classes every Saturday morning at the New York School of the Theatre and following her graduation from Julia Richman, went to the American Academy of Dramatic Arts for a year. The stage eluded her, and the nearest she got to it was an usher's job at the St. James Theatre on West Forty-Fourth Street.

Her stylish looks led to a few modeling jobs, and in time, she landed on the cover of *Vogue*.

This particular cover caught the eye of Nancy "Slim" Hawks, who was then married to Howard Hawks, one of the best film directors of the day. Slim was herself an extraordinarily attractive and bright young lady. She looked at the model and arranged a meeting between her and Howard Hawks, who got Warner Brothers to sign her to a joint contract with him. She was seventeen and off to Hollywood.

Katherine Higgins, who was the manager of the Warner Brothers studio commissary, said, "All I know is that when Lauren came into the studio Green Room Restaurant the first few times, everybody stopped eating and talking and just looked. In Hollywood, that's success."

Miss Higgins may have thought so, but it was not to happen for a while.

Betty was growing more and more impatient. At seventeen, one does not enjoy inactivity. She haunted the office of her agent, Charlie Feldman. He tried to reassure her by saying that Howard Hawks definitely had something in mind for her. Whenever she and Hawks met, he would narrow his eyes and study her and say, "I see you with either Humphrey Bogart or Cary Grant."

Later on, she often wondered what would have happened if she had made a movie with Cary Grant, rather than with Humphrey Bogart.

Perc Westmore, who was the head of Warner Brothers makeup department, predicted Bacall's success early on, saying: "She has the indescribable qualities that Dietrich and Garbo had when they first appeared in Hollywood. Like them, she may not be startlingly beautiful, but she'll never go unnoticed in any company. She has what it takes to become great on the screen, and there isn't much my department can do to add to that."

Finally, Hawks made a test of her for his upcoming picture based on Hemingway's novel TO HAVE AND HAVE NOT—the celebrated whistle scene. A few days later, Hawks took her down onto the set to introduce her to Bogart, who was shooting PASSAGE TO MARSEILLES. They exchanged conversational how-do-you-do's and looked each other over. A few days later, Lauren was waiting in Hawks's outer office when Bogart came out. He looked at her and said, "I just saw your test. We'll have a lot of fun together." Prophetic, indeed.

Howard Hawks said afterward about Bogart: "He was really underrated as an actor. Without his help, I couldn't have done what I did with Bacall. Not many actors would sit around and wait while a girl steals a scene. But he fell in love with the girl and the girl with him, and that made it easy."

"I don't believe in competitive acting," Bogart once said. "I remember Alfred Lunt once said that he didn't either. 'If I did,' Alfred Lunt said, 'Lynn and I would be billed as Lunt versus Fontanne.' "

From his screen image, it would be difficult to guess that Humphrey Bogart was extremely well born and bred. His father was a

To Have and Have Not *1944*

Key Largo *1948*

The Big Sleep   *1946*

The Big Sleep   *1946*

Key Largo   *1948*

To Have and Have Not   *1944*

distinguished New York doctor; his mother was Maud Humphrey, a famous portrait painter who specialized in society children. He was educated mainly at private schools and at Phillips Andover Academy.

Bogart became part of the pool of young leading men and knocked about the theatre, playing in flops, going on the road, working as a replacement in a hit. Not until Robert E. Sherwood cast him as the killer, Duke Mantee, in THE PETRIFIED FOREST did Bogart score heavily. He then re-created his part in the film version. That got him one of the leads in DEAD END, and his Hollywood career sparked and took off. (He had already had a preliminary movie career, but it had fizzled out: A DEVIL WITH WOMEN, UP THE RIVER, BODY AND SOUL, BAD SISTER, WOMEN OF ALL NATIONS, A HOLY TERROR, LOVE AFFAIR, BIG CITY BLUES, THREE ON A MATCH, and MIDNIGHT.)

Off screen, Humphrey Bogart was a man of strong opinions and admirable principles. He once wrote:

> If any actors think they can't express their political opinions freely and keep their jobs, they're either seeing bogymen or have the wrong kind of bosses. I'm inclined to think it is the former.
> It may be a moot question what good, except to their own souls, actors, painters, musicians and members of kindred artistic professions may accomplish by participating in politics. We may be giddy dopes or impractical dreamers incapable of coping with down-to-earth problems of governing ourselves. Only I seem to recall a distinguished gentleman by the name of Ignace Paderewski, who not only was the world's greatest concert pianist but a great enough patriot—and politician—to serve with distinction as prime minister and minister of foreign affairs of his native Poland.

During the making of TO HAVE AND HAVE NOT, Bogart, the famous tough guy, was considerate and helpful and kind to the young beginner, Bacall.

The crew began to notice that they were chatting endlessly between takes and that frequently, instead of going to the commissary for lunch, they would go off and picnic on the back lot.

There was something going there, all right. Howard Hawks noticing this, had the writers begin to add scenes and to build them into a TEAM.

"The kind of chemistry they had," he said, "is something you can't create and you can't buy. It's either there or it isn't."

Success, however, turned out to be as great a burden as the effort to make it.

Imagine going out on a publicity tour and being preceded by a handout that contained the following:

> Arresting describes her appearance better than beautiful. In a metropolitan crowd or on a deserted desert, she'd stand out, and draw encore gazes. She has long, lithe legs, curves in the right places, and the proper proportions. Her mouth is wide and generous, smiles easily and challengingly. Her blonde hair has a tawny tint, and her blue-green eyes mirror cool, calm intelligence. When she speaks, her low throaty voice commands immediate attention, completes a perfect personality ensemble.

It was during the trip to New York to promote TO HAVE AND HAVE NOT that Lauren faced her first press conference. Gossip about her and Bogart had preceded her. She arrived by train at Grand Central Station and was met by a horde of reporters and photographers, as well as eight Warner Brothers press agents.

Her entrance to New York on this occasion was in sharp dramatic contrast to her exit only two and a half years before.

In the circumstances, she handled herself admirably. A part of the press conference was reported as follows:

FIRST REPORTER:

Well, are you going to marry the guy?

BACALL:

What guy?

FIRST REPORTER:

Come on—Bogart, of course.

BACALL:

I'd like to wait till he asks me.

SECOND REPORTER:

Hasn't he asked you?

BACALL:

All I know about this is what I read in the papers. I haven't seen him for three weeks.

THIRD REPORTER:

You mean he hasn't said anything about marriage?

BACALL:

That's right. He hasn't said anything. In the last three weeks.

FOURTH REPORTER:

You mean he asked you before that?

BACALL:

Look, all kidding aside, you wouldn't want me to give away a trade secret, would you?

FIRST REPORTER:

That's what I want to know. Is this strictly promotion or is it on the level?

BACALL:

You'll have to ask him. He started this. Let him finish it. I can't.

FIFTH REPORTER:

Do you love him?

BACALL:

That's the sixty-four dollar question.

FIFTH REPORTER:

Do you admire him?

BACALL:

I think he's wonderful. He's been swell to me.

FIRST REPORTER:

Would you marry him if he asked you?

BACALL:

You're kind of pinning me down. I don't want to answer, and I don't want to lie. Can't a girl have any secrets?

Within a year, Humphrey Bogart and Lauren Bacall were man and wife and con-tinuing a beautiful partnership on and off the screen. The success of TO HAVE AND HAVE NOT and the TEAM was so great that the studio lost no time in putting them into another picture as soon as it could be readied.

While that picture was being prepared, Bogart made CONFLICT, and Lauren made CONFIDENTIAL AGENT.

Then together again in THE BIG SLEEP; and afterward, although between their TEAM pictures, Bogart made DEAD RECKONING, THE TWO MRS. CARROLLS, and THE TREASURE OF SIERRA MADRE, Lauren Bacall was reserved for the TEAM and did nothing until DARK PASSAGE, and finally, KEY LARGO.

The relationship they created, the tension, the give-and-take, was of high order and endlessly fascinating.

In 1955, they were announced for a movie called MELVILLE GOODWIN, U.S.A. Preparations began and production was almost under way when Bogart fell ill. He was not to recover, and died in 1957.

There is hardly a player who lives in death as strongly as he does. The manager of the New Yorker Theater, who ran a Humphrey Bogart festival, reports that on the day he played THE BIG SLEEP and TO HAVE AND HAVE NOT as a double feature: "I had two hundred people sitting on the floor. It was wild. I had to turn away a couple of thousand people. And that audience! The first time Bogie appeared, they cheered, and that was just the beginning."

And recently, the program director of a Chicago television station specializing in movie programming said to me: "Whenever my ratings start to go down a little, I throw on a few Bogarts, and they bounce right back again."

The TEAM of Humphrey Bogart and Lauren Bacall was so integrated, so close, and so powerful, that something of the fabulous Bogart image remains with Lauren Bacall even now. The aura of charming hardness, daring audaciousness, healthy cynicism, and basic good humor emanates from the survivor of this terrific TEAM.

WRONG TEAMS

Tab Hunter and Sophia Loren   That Kind of Woman   *1959*

James Stewart and Paulette Goddard   Pot o' Gold   *1941*

Katharine Hepburn and Bob Hope The Iron Petticoat *1956*

Greer Garson and Clark Gable Adventure *1945*

Road to Morocco   1942

The Nonchalants
BOB HOPE and BING CROSBY

A TEAM composed of one man and one woman is far easier to analyze than those composed of man-man or woman-woman. Consider Bob Hope and Bing Crosby.

This TEAM created itself in the late thirties. At that time, Bing was a Paramount star in films. He also had one of the most popular radio shows of the era, the Kraft Music Hall. In addition, he made scarcely a record that did not hit the Top Ten almost at once.

Bob Hope, too, was a rising comedian at Paramount.

They became off-screen chums. They shared a number of common interests, the principal one being golf, at which they became amicable competitors at the Lakeside Golf Club.

In 1939, Bing appeared in three big hits: EAST SIDE OF HEAVEN, PARIS HONEYMOON, and THE STAR MAKER.

Bob Hope's career up to this point was confined to doing small parts and supporting specialties.

Bob Hope, brilliant and aggressive, knew he could make it if given the chance. He believed in himself, but above all, he knew that he had to be seen, and so he would appear at benefits, studio parties, charity bazaars, anywhere and everywhere he could get a platform, a spotlight, and perhaps a musician or two.

At one of these benefits, Bing Crosby also appeared. Somehow they found themselves on the stage together. They began clowning about, imitating each other, exchanging barbs, and the audience ate it up. Before long, they had become a benefit TEAM.

Then came a big show, put on at the Del Mar Race Track. It was at this affair that Bing coined the nickname "Ski Nose" for Hope, and Hope in turn took it out on Crosby's unsuccessful race horses. They finished with a song and the old soft shoe.

Harlan Thompson, then a Paramount producer, was in the audience. He had had a great career on Broadway as a lyricist and librettist. Among his shows was LITTLE JESSIE JAMES, and the song "I Love You," for which he provided the lyrics. It was Thompson who perceived that Crosby and Hope had viable chemistry. When he took his idea to the Paramount brass, he was turned down. "No contrast," said one. "Crosby needs a girl," said another, "and Hope needs a straight man. Crosby ain't gonna be a straight man for anybody."

"He's right," added a third. "You can't have a team with two comics."

Thompson argued his case, citing Laurel and Hardy, reminding them of such successful TEAMS as Victor McLaglen and Edmund Lowe. But the answer was no.

Undeterred, Harlan Thompson discussed his idea with two of the brightest writers on the lot, Frank Butler and Don Hartman (who later would become head of the studio). They came up with a script called THE ROAD TO SINGAPORE and cleverly included a part for the studio's current sexpot, Dorothy Lamour.

What the imagination of the front office was not able to see was provided by the concrete quality of a shooting script, and the picture went forward. It opened in April 1940, and it was clear that a sensational box office TEAM had been launched.

Don Hartman said: "You can throw a piece of gum on a map of the world and make a Road picture anywhere it sticks."

The second movie was called THE ROAD TO ZANZIBAR, at which point the United States became involved in World War II and Bob Hope became the most peripatetic entertainer the world has ever known.

Between trips, he stopped long enough to join Bing in making THE ROAD TO MOROCCO.

In 1943, Bing and Bob and Dorothy made THE ROAD TO UTOPIA.

Their activities were not confined, however, to their TEAM pictures. Along the way, Crosby interspersed IF I HAD MY WAY, RHYTHM ON THE RIVER, BIRTH OF THE BLUES, HOLIDAY INN, DIXIE, STAR SPANGLED RHYTHM, GOING MY WAY (for which he won an Academy Award), THE BELLS OF ST. MARY'S, opposite Ingrid Bergman.

Meanwhile, Hope appeared in THE GHOST BREAKERS and MY FAVORITE BLONDE.

But whatever else they did, the Road pictures had become a solid staple of Paramount programming. In 1947, THE ROAD TO RIO. In 1952, THE ROAD TO BALI. In 1962, THE ROAD TO HONG KONG. The set on these pictures was al-

Road to Rio *1948*

Road to Rio *1948*

Road to Hong Kong *1962*

Road to Rio *1948*

Road to Hong Kong *1962*

Publicity shot

Road to Hong Kong *1962*

Road to Hong Kong *1962*

Road to Rio *1948*

Road to Hong Kong *1962*

Road to Morocco *1942*

Road to Rio *1948*

Road to Singapore *1940*

Road to Utopia *1945*

ways chaotic. Teams of gag writers, sometimes as many as a dozen, standing by and popping ideas for lines and jokes and bits of business and ad libs.

What Crosby and Hope developed was an amiable, all-American kind of feud, unknown in other cultures.

Good friends do not insult each other in France, nor do they rib one another unmercifully in England, but the whole approach was so fresh and original and, above all, funny, that it worked and continued to work for years.

Time magazine summed it up: "The road shows were rummage sales of stuff out of vaudeville, burlesque—marvelously shoddy masterpieces of farce and fantasy, stitched together with clichés and ad libs. The series proved, if nothing else, that Crosby was nearly as deft—and daft—a comedian as Hope. But by then, Bing was a giant with or without Hope."

Harry Lillis Crosby was born in Tacoma, Washington, on May 2, 1904. He was one of a large family created by Harry Lowe Crosby and the former Katherine Helen Harrigan. Harry was the fourth of five sons, and there were also two daughters.

The family soon moved to Spokane, where Father went to work for the Inland Brewery Company and did well until Prohibition wiped the company out. The brewery was turned into a pickle factory, and Harry Lillis, already nicknamed "Bing," worked there for a while. Both parents were musical, and all the kids were given lessons in instruments of their choice.

The Spokane *Spokesman-Review* carried on Sundays a rotogravure section and a full-color comic section. One of the strips was called "The Bingville Bugle." The hero of the cartoon was a character named Bingo, whom the cartoonist had given outsized ears. One of Harry's playmates, Valentine Hobart, noticed that Harry's ears were rather large and so he began calling Harry Bingo. Then in the way that prepubescent people shorten things, Bingo became Bing and remained so.

Bing went to a Jesuit school that had an exceptionally good course in elocution. He became a good athlete, worked every summer at various jobs he loathed, until at sixteen, he landed one backstage at the Auditorium Theater in Spokane. It was here that the virulent stage bug bit him. When he went back to school that fall to Gonzaga University, he formed a band called the Musicaladers. Bing was the drummer. Another member of the group was Al Rinker, who some years later would still be with Bing as one of the Rhythm Boys.

Al Rinker's sister was the great American jazz singer, Mildred Bailey. Bing Crosby and Al Rinker developed a singing act that became so successful that they were eventually signed as a specialty act by the great Paul Whiteman. Along the way, they met a piano player named Harry Barris. The duo became a trio known as the Rhythm Boys and became a standard part of Paul Whiteman's act.

In time, they left Whiteman and went to try their luck in Hollywood.

The trio proved to be unwieldy and soon split up.

Nothing is so powerful as a crooner who has met his time. The talkies were new. Musical films were the rage, and Bing Crosby's beautiful, velvet, mellifluous voice recorded perfectly.

He built a marvelously varied career, playing not only in musicals but dramas such as LITTLE BOY LOST, THE COUNTRY GIRL, and STAGECOACH, and although he was somewhat self-deprecating about his acting ability—"I do two kinds of acting: loud and soft"—he was a far better actor than he knew or was willing to admit.

It is probably fair to say that in his teaming with his great friend Hope, he was at his freest, most relaxed, and ultimately was at his happiest.

Bob Hope was born in London, England. When, is anyone's guess, since he has always kept the date of his birth a secret. He appeared for years in vaudeville, and eventually made a Broadway debut in ROBERTA. He then appeared in a late edition of the Ziegfeld Follies and as the lead opposite Ethel Merman in RED, HOT AND BLUE. Simultaneously, he did a successful radio series.

His first movie was at Paramount, called THE BIG BROADCAST OF 1938. Then COLLEGE SWING, GIVE ME A SAILOR, THANKS FOR THE MEMORY, NEVER SAY DIE, SOME LIKE IT HOT, THE CAT AND THE CANARY.

From this list, it can be seen that had he not had the great good fortune at this point to be teamed with Bing Crosby, his movie career might easily have expired. But the Crosby-Hope combination kept him in hits and before the public, and he was able to add movies of his own, such as LOUISIANA PURCHASE, THE PALEFACE, FANCY PANTS, MY FAVORITE SPY, THAT CERTAIN FEELING, and BEAU JAMES, in which he played Jimmy Walker.

Perhaps without realizing it, their on-screen and off-screen relationship led them to imitations of each other. As one watches the Road pictures and then their individual pictures, one can see that they picked up, unconsciously perhaps, from one another gestures, attitudes, takes, looks, and so on. Thus in the end, there was some Crosby in Hope and some Hope in Crosby. And it all fitted and it was all fine. Moreover, they created something absolutely original and inimitable.

Two classy entertainers merged into the classiest of TEAMS.

The Awful Truth *1937*

High Comedy
IRENE DUNNE and CARY GRANT

When I directed them in MY FAVORITE WIFE in 1939, they had made only one previous film—THE AWFUL TRUTH, a delightful Leo McCarey concoction. Yet their teamwork gave the impression of a lifetime partnership, such as that of Alfred Lunt and Lynn Fontanne.

They conveyed the notion that life was a fascinating game—best when played by evenly matched adversaries, but not always according to the rules. They seemed to understand each other and to forgive even that.

"We do not love our friends in spite of their faults," wrote Montaigne, "but *because* of their faults."

Sam and Bella Spewack, the authors of the screenplay—and themselves a sophisticated married couple—understood perfectly the underlying elements of the Dunne-Grant relationship and wrote for it with great effectiveness.

The idea that TEAMS are best composed of contrasting personalities is exploded by the success of Irene Dunne and Cary Grant. From almost every point of view, their screen personae are alike: culturally, intellectually, morally, economically, emotionally. The only real difference between them is that he is male and she is the opposite, and that becomes the conflicting element to exploit to the full.

Moreover, in their playing they seem always to have some private, unspoken (perhaps unspeakable?) joke going between them.

I can attest that they really enjoyed acting together, and this quality is apparent in every scene, isn't it?

"Acting with Irene," Cary once said to me, "is very like a long, continuing, never-ending flirtation. She's constantly surprising, and that makes every hour of every day working with her—if you can call it working—a joy. Getting up at six in the morning, driving to the studio—make-up—wardrobe—putting on a dinner jacket and playing a scene on Stage Twelve that's actually supposed to be happening at night, in Manhattan—now, that's not really something a man looks forward to. But whenever Irene is involved in it with me, I look forward to it and I find myself driving to the studio faster than usual."

When I repeated what he had said to Irene, she giggled, blushed charmingly, and said, "Oh, that Cary! Do you suppose he means it? I certainly hope so—because I feel exactly the same about him. I'm always so confident when we're working together. I know that he's not going to make one false step, and if I do, he'll be there to steady me. I've never known—on stage or screen—a more generous actor, or a more stimulating partner. I have no idea what makes us a team. That thing called chemistry, I suppose, that no one seems to be able to define. No, I can't possibly put it into words—what makes us a team. All I know is I'm delighted that we are."

"The trouble with this year is," complained producer Arthur Freed, "you've got a lot of tuxedo scripts and no tuxedo actors!"

There had, indeed, been a spate of high comedies, and casting the rash of imitations proved to be a problem. Cary Grant *was* "a tuxedo actor"—one of the few. But for that exalted position, he had been made, not born.

I knew him first as Archie Leach, a friend of my friend, Moss Hart. He was handsome. So what? Handsome is a dime a dozen around show business always. What else was he? A seasoned and experienced stilt walker. "Didn't you see him in that great English act? He was the one on the tallest stilts." He had come down finally and gone to work for the Shuberts—those inevitable Shuberts—as a chorus boy, bit player, featured actor, and finally, leading man, in various musicals and operettas.

Now he was around, looking for work with not much equipment other than his striking good looks.

We all knew that it was a matter of time before he would make it to Hollywood—*to* Hollywood, but would he make it *in* Hollywood? That was the question.

He had certainly come a long way from Bristol, England, where he was born on January 18, 1904—but would he continue his journey to the stars?

Sitting around on the set between takes, Cary would sometimes talk of his difficult, Dickensian beginnings. There was much of his story, I confess, that I did not believe. There

142

My Favorite Wife 1940

Penny Serenade *1941*

Penny Serenade *1941*

were scenes that seemed too stereotyped, overly dramatic, stretching credibility. But as time passed, I have found that everything he told me was true: his mother going mad from the strain of poverty and being institutionalized; his movie-struck childhood; joining an acrobatic troupe as a boy; his first trip to the United States at sixteen with the Pender Troupe. On board the S.S. *Olympic,* he sees Mary Pickford and Douglas Fairbanks. They are on their honeymoon. Fairbanks is his out-and-out, all-time idol. The man, the star, the being he wished to emulate, perhaps because Fairbanks was an accomplished athlete, too. Cary says that his predilection for the deep tan he has always affected probably stems from his desire to copy Douglas Fairbanks.

Playing the Hippodrome—then the largest theatre in all the world—the troupe flops and returns to England, but he stays on in New York City. He is eighteen. Tough going. The time he worked at Coney Island as a boardwalk stilt walker for Steeplechase Park. Moving in with a struggling designer named Orry-Kelly and peddling Orry's hand-painted neckties all over town. Orry, who, by 1939, was one of the most successful designers in Hollywood, visits the set one day and releases a flood of memories. Awful stories of deprivation and scrounging and rejection, which now can be laughed at. The Shubert days. BOOM BOOM, in 1929.

Cary gets the lead in A WONDERFUL NIGHT (a version of DIE FLEDERMAUS), and it opens just as the stock market crashes, emptying theatres everywhere. And what about that summer, doing RIO RITA and COUNTESS MARITZA in the open air in St. Louis, and competing with the mosquitoes? Hanging around Rudley's, a third-rate restaurant at Broadway and 41st Street with Moss and Preston Sturges and Bogart and George Murphy. And his trip to Hollywood by car, strictly on spec, against all advice. Then getting a test and landing a contract with B. P. Shulberg at Paramount less than a week after his arrival. The studio doesn't like his name: Leach. "Who wants to see a leech?" Archie came up with "Cary Lockwood."

"Too long," they said.

"Cary *Grant?*"

"Okay."

In his first year at Paramount, he made seven movies, playing opposite Sylvia Sidney, Carole Lombard, Tallulah Bankhead, Marlene Dietrich, Nancy Carroll, and others—getting nowhere. Then the super-camp movies with Mae West.

"How could *anyone* be Mae West's leading man?" he once recalled. "She was her *own* leading man!"

But in SHE DONE HIM WRONG and I'M NO ANGEL, Cary tried.

In his first three years in Hollywood, he

Penny Serenade *1941*

My Favorite Wife *1940*

made seventeen films, all of them eminently forgettable.

In 1935, at last a break. Orry-Kelly's friend, George Cukor, was planning a British background film to be called SYLVIA SCARLETT. Orry suggested Cary. Cukor and his star took a chance and cast Cary Grant in the lead. The picture, a mad comedy far ahead of its time, was not a success, but Cary with the assistance of Katharine Hepburn's characteristic generosity and Cukor's brilliant perception of Grant's possibilities, scored mightily.

And still there followed two years of mediocrity: BIG BROWN EYES, SUZY, WEDDING PRESENT, WHEN YOU'RE IN LOVE, THE TOAST OF NEW YORK —but then came TOPPER, a tuxedo picture and a splendid one. His performance in this gave Leo McCarey the idea of giving him the lead opposite Irene Dunne in THE AWFUL TRUTH, and by extension, a career.

Cary Grant will cheerfully admit that Leo McCarey furnished him with more than a part —he gave him a character, a personality, an image, one that he uses to this day.

Irene Dunne brought her own. She had been in pictures since 1930, with a debut in LEATHERNECKING, followed by the tremendous epic western success, CIMARRON. The surprise was that she had been brought out as a result of her stage successes in musicals, and here she

was a hit in a drama. It was years before she got a musical, and finally a comedy—THEODORA GOES WILD—surprising everyone in the business again. Meanwhile she had plowed her way through (among others) SYMPHONY OF SIX MILLION, BACK STREET, THE SILVER CORD, ANN VICKERS, and THE AGE OF INNOCENCE.

From their first appearance in the opening scene of THE AWFUL TRUTH, it was easily apparent that they were meant for each other.

They are a couple in a courtroom, splitting up. The custody of their little dog is at issue. Irene is charming the judge (and the audience) with her recital of how they acquired the little dog in the first place. Cary tries to interject his version, but is reduced by her vitality to grunts and squeaks.

Finally, the impatient judge speaks. "I'll take it under advisement," he says.

Cary wants to say something, but the judge cuts him off sharply and repeats, "I'll take it *under advisement*."

"Yeah," says Cary, "but when will you *know?*"

I do not wish to emulate the lady I overheard say, "I love that Robert Montgomery. He's always got a comeback," but in the case of the above scene, the rollicking fadeout was almost entirely a triumph of personality and delivery.

The Dunne-Grant TEAM delighted audi-

Penny Serenade *1941*

Penny Serenade *1941*

Penny Serenade *1941*

Penny Serenade *1941*

Penny Serenade *1941*

The Awful Truth *1937*

ences who clamored to see them again, but it was to be three years before they next played together, in MY FAVORITE WIFE.

A few days before shooting was to begin, Cary came up to my office at RKO to see me. After an hour or more of bubbling enthusiasm about our project, he got up to leave and said gravely, "You know about the left side of my face, don't you?"

"No."

"It's dead."

"Dead?"

"Absolutely. Please don't photograph it. You'll get nothing. It's dead."

I scanned his face, taking a step closer, and put my attention on that left side. "It looks all right to me," I said.

He regarded me grimly and said, "I know what I'm talking about. It's dead. Don't photograph it! Promise?"

"Promise," I heard myself echo.

For the next two days, I pondered the technical questions that this promise posed.

The day before we were to begin, William Hawks, Miss Dunne's agent, came in to see me to wish me luck.

"You've read her contract, haven't you?" he asked.

"Of course not. How could I? They don't show me stars' contracts."

"Oh." He looked troubled. "I'd have thought they'd've told you."

"Told me what?"

"About her left side. You're supposed to stay off it as much as you can. I mean to say, she's not unreasonable, but if you want to keep her happy, no left side."

He was gone.

On the first day of shooting, there we were: Cary, Irene, Rudy Maté, the cameraman, the set, the crew.

I paced about the set slowly and deliberately for twenty minutes, seemingly deep in thought, stopping now and then to frame a shot through my fingers, then shaking my head and pacing again, but saying nothing. I could see Cary worrying that he was involved with a nut.

I noticed Irene whispering something to my assistant. The studio production manager was sent for. A tough guy, J. R. Crone.

"What the hell's goin' on here?" Crone demanded.

There was a hush. I spoke softly and seriously. "I've been told to stay off Mr. Grant's left side," I said. "Also off Miss Dunne's left side—I'm just trying to figure out where to put the fucking camera."

MY FAVORITE WIFE began in a burst of wild laughter.

Working with these two was a joy—both so professional and prepared, cooperative and unselfish—that I longed to repeat the experience.

On a trip to France, I found a story called PASSPORT TO LIFE. A shady racketeer, on board the *Normandy*, meets a young woman who works for an agency finding homes for war-orphaned children. The racketeer falls for her and gathers that the way to this one's heart (or whatever) is through her work. He adopts a refugee child—and then discovers America through the eyes of the little boy. In the end he becomes eligible not only for a partnership in a shipboard romance but for life.

I engaged Dorothy Parker and Alan Campbell to write the screenplay, and we appeared to be underway. I gave the story to Cary. He loved it.

"My God, what a story!" he said to me the morning after I had given it to him. "You know what happened to me? I read it in bed—last night—right through. And you know what? My God, what a story. I couldn't get to sleep for twenty minutes!"

Dear Cary.

Irene liked it, too, but I was drafted before we could get it off the ground, and it joined the vast morass of untold dreams.

Their next film together was PENNY SERENADE, a moving story of adoption, directed by George Stevens. Many times subsequently, Irene Dunne and Cary Grant wanted to be together in a film, but it was not to be.

Still, they are fondly remembered as a pair, a short marriage, but a lovely, rich, and rewarding one. Unique, too. And as the legendary Martha Graham says, "The unique must be fulfilled."

Penny Serenade *1941*

High jinks at Pickfair

DOUGLAS FAIRBANKS and MARY PICKFORD

Douglas Fairbanks. Mary Pickford. Pickfair. A heady combination that fuses into that most ineffable of all qualities—glamour.

Would it have the same magic if it read "Douglas Ulman, Gladys Smith, 1143 Summit Drive"?

Glamour, one perceives, is made, not born, and in Douglas Fairbanks-Mary Pickford we have perhaps the outstanding glamour manufacturers of the twentieth century. They have been called "the most popular couple the world has known." At first glance, this would appear to be rather steamy hyperbole—but think for a minute. If they were not, who were?

When I first conceived the idea of exploring the great movie TEAMS in an attempt to discover the magic formula that made them great, I began to make a list. The first pair to appear on that list was Fairbanks and Pickford. Of course.

Months later, I discovered to my astonishment, that Douglas Fairbanks and Mary Pickford had made exactly *one* film together. *One!* And that one a colossal failure—THE TAMING OF THE SHREW.

Show business hindsight is a feckless perspective, and only tyros or smartasses indulge in it. Greatness in the arts being a voyage of discovery, it is an easy matter to get lost, to founder, to be shipwrecked.

Once, during a tax examination by a hawkeye representing the Internal Revenue Service, I was asked, "Now this play you put on with Spencer Tracy—"

"*The Rugged Path.*"

"Yes."

"By Robert E. Sherwood?"

"Yes. Now that was a failure."

"Alas."

"And occupied you for—how long?"

"About six months."

"That's right. And generated just about nil."

"Well, we all took cuts, and so on."

"Now what I don't understand is this. Didn't you know it wouldn't go?"

"Of course not."

"You mean you knew it would?"

"No. I didn't know."

"Well, if you didn't know, why did you do it?"

I did not answer the unanswerable question. How could I?

Certainly, Fairbanks and Pickford thought THE TAMING OF THE SHREW would be the crowning glory of their professional life. In the face of the disaster it turned out to be, it is easy to ask: What made them think they could make a successful Shakespearean film when no one ever had? What persuaded them that they could play Shakespeare without training or background in the classics? Why did they choose Sam Taylor to direct and permit him to take the hilarious credit line: "With additional dialogue by Sam Taylor"? Having hired the illustrious Constance Collier to coach Mary, why did they permit Taylor to fire her? Why did Doug fail to learn his lines and use blackboards? Why did all concerned later place the blame on someone else? Doug and Mary blamed each other.

There are those who believe that it was this mountainous catastrophe that presaged their separation about three years later and their subsequent divorce. The fairy tale was over and seemed askew, with its unhappy ending. In 1933, Kings and Queens did not divorce—and the Doug-Mary TEAM was about as close to the idea of royalty as Americans ever got.

Why did they make only one movie together? I asked Sam Goldwyn, the only survivor of the original United Artists company still at work in America.

"Because they were crazy," he said. "And you know what kind of crazy? Money crazy. I tell you, how those two could spend money, you wouldn't believe it. Around the world six, seven times, and each time with a whole troupe. Not only maids and valets and secretaries—but friends and guests. Dozens. And Pickfair. Some place. There was a time you couldn't get in there without blue blood. Every night the table was set for sixteen, and dinner prepared. You know why?"

"No."

"Guess."

"I can't."

"Because he would sometimes come home

The Taming of the Shrew   *1929*

and bring a whole bunch with him. And sometimes not. He was the most charming man I ever met in my life. But a little crazy. So spending like that meant they had to earn like that. Oh, how they worked. And many times the subject came up at the board meetings: We would sit and try to make good plans—Charlie and Griffith and them and me. And whenever it came up—the subject that they should work together—they would thumbs-down it. Why? Because they said each one was such a big star that going in the same picture was like wasting one of them. Doug used to say, 'There's only so many seats in a theatre, and once you've got an ass in each one, that's it. Show me how to get two asses into every seat, and we'll do one together.' He could be very vulgar sometimes, Doug—but the most charming. He was like a big kid, you know. Never grew up. All that jumping from balconies and climbing trees and daredevil—kid stuff. And Mary? Boy, was she a business woman—making a deal with her, you would sweat—you would spit cotton by the time you were done. People say I'm a tough businessman—they should make a deal with Mary. But on the screen? Who was ever better? These little pisspots we got now? Mary was Mary, and when they called her America's Sweetheart, you know why? Because, f'Crissake —she *was!* Those were *some* days!"

Charlie Chaplin said that he was first introduced to Mary Pickford by his friend and leading lady, Mabel Normand, who said, "Charlie, I want you to meet Hetty Green— alias Mary Pickford."

And he further recounts the bizarre joy of watching the petite, sweet, demure creature at a U.A. board meeting, tossing about references to amortizations and deferred stocks and legal discrepancies and page eight, para. B, line seven.

It had begun early. When D. W. Griffith engaged her at the age of sixteen, he told her that the pay would be five dollars a day. "Ten," she countered.

"We pay everyone five."

"I'm a Belasco actress," she insisted. "Ten."

D. W. finally gave in, but told her to keep it dark. At the end of each day, she got five dollars from the paymaster and five dollars from D. W.'s pocket. Here she was again haggling with D. W., but the five dollars had become five million. No wonder she ended in luxury and splendor, while D. W. Griffith died destitute in a single room at the Hollywood Knickerbocker Hotel.

Mary Pickford was born Gladys Smith in Toronto on April 8, 1893, and made her stage debut on September 19, 1898—which would make her about five and a half years old. By the time she was eight, she was a local favorite. EAST LYNNE. And at nine, a star. UNCLE TOM'S CABIN.

In the beginning, she was not the only theatrical figure in the family; her younger sister and brother, Lottie and Jack, were also part of Mrs. Pickford's troupe—and at times Mrs. Pickford herself made appearances. But it was Gladys who virtually supported the family.

It has been widely reported that David Belasco "discovered" Gladys Smith and renamed her Mary Pickford—it is true that he changed her name, but he did not discover her. She discovered him.

In New York, she knocked about, looking for work, heard about Belasco, found that he was doing a play called THE WARRENS OF VIRGINIA and that there was a part in it for a young girl. She haunted his theatre and his offices daily—at all hours—until she succeeded in getting an audition. The result was a sixteen-month engagement in THE WARRENS OF VIRGINIA. She was now "a Belasco actress."

But stage roles were sparse for child actresses at the time and at sixteen Mary found herself at the Biograph Company, at 11 East 14th Street. There she met D. W. Griffith, who tested her and engaged her. A film career that was to last for twenty-four years had begun.

She had little faith in the rather raffish new medium, partly as a result of her first exposure to it a few months earlier in Chicago. She strongly disapproved of Lottie and Jack going to New York nickelodeons, even though they pointed out that as kids they got in two for a nickel. But in Chicago, one afternoon, bored and curious, she paid ten cents (!) to see "Hale's Tours and Scenes of the World"—a special attraction shown in a fake railroad car.

As the flickering landscapes came on, the car began to rock as though in motion, and Mary became violently trainsick.

Between 1909 and 1912, Mary Pickford made 143 short films and one long mistake: a marriage to Oliver Moore, a handsome, talented lush.

By 1913, she was a well-known film player, but David Belasco reminded her that she had promised him, in gratitude, to come back and work for him whenever he wanted or needed her. Now he did, for a play called THE GOOD LITTLE DEVIL, with Ernest Truex and Lillian Gish.

Back to the movies again—but not for Griffith, who refused to pay her more than $300 a week. Adolph Zukor gave her $500, and she went to work for Famous Players.

In 1915, Mary and her husband went to lunch at Elsie Janis's house in Tarrytown—where she met for the first time an actor she had often admired on the stage, Douglas Fairbanks.

Douglas Elton Ulman was the son of Ella Adelaide Marsh Fairbanks Wilcox Ulman by her third husband, Hezekiah Charles Ulman, a New York lawyer who had represented her in the divorce proceedings against her second husband, Edward Wilcox. Douglas, her third son (one by each husband), was born in Denver, Colorado, on May 23, 1883. He was unpopular from the start with his southern belle mother (although some records indicate her birthplace as New York City). "Mother would reach down in the baby carriage and pull the blanket over my face when she saw somebody coming." The reason? She thought that the dark-skinned infant looked like his father—Jewish. Up to this time, she had successfully concealed this dreaded Semite skeleton in the family closet. But the skeleton had a valuable pragmatic side—he loved the theatre, went often, and took the family. He was a friend of Edwin Booth, whom he resembled. Young Doug was stagestruck early on. As he grew older, the condition intensified, and Ella was dismayed that even his baptism by the great Archbishop Joseph P. Machebeuf at the Im-

maculate Conception Church had failed to erase the stain of his birth.

When Douglas was five, Ulman disappeared on a wave of alcohol and was not seen by the family again for about seven years. At that time, Ulman accosted his son, Douglas, on a Denver street and took him to a bar for a man-to-man drink and talk. He urged Douglas to go on the stage—"and not end up a tosspot like me, my boy. Let's have one more."

Douglas took him home, hoping for a reconciliation. It failed. Ella threw Charlie out and lost no time in taking Douglas to the Denver headquarters of the Women's Christian Temperance Union, where he took the pledge. By and large, he stuck to it for a lifetime.

At sixteen, he was a handsome ham, given to acting on his school stage whenever he could and off-stage all the time.

At that age, he left Denver and school and made his way to New York—specifically Broadway and fame and fortune.

Frederick Warde, a minor touring British player, was a friend of Doug's father—his only theatre contact. Doug looked him up, and to his amazement, was hired by him.

On September 11, 1899, Douglas Fairbanks opened with the Frederick Warde Company as Florio in THE DUKE'S JESTER.

After a long tour, he returned to Broadway and alternated between stage jobs and odd jobs—some of them very odd indeed, according to his accounts. Finally, he was a chorus boy for Lee Shubert in FANTANA, a Japanese operetta.

Grace George and her husband, William Brady, saw the opening night. Miss George was celebrated for her eye for talent, and her eye caught Doug. His athletic prowess charmed Brady—a sports promotor turned producer. He signed Douglas to a five-year contract, starting at $40 a week, and Fairbanks was well and truly on his way. He began in A CASE OF FRENZIED FINANCE, went on to CLOTHES ($50 a week), and then THE PIT. Now a near disaster. Marriage to a society girl, Beth Sully, whose father, a tycoon, persuaded him to leave the stage and become an executive in the Buchan Soap Company, which had its headquarters in the Flatiron Building.

Douglas Fairbanks carries Mary Pickford through an admiring crowd.

Birth of United Artists, 1919: (front, from left) D. W. Griffith, Mary Pickford, Charlie Chaplin, Douglas Fairbanks; lawyers at back.

A few months of this was enough. He moved with his wife into the Algonquin Hotel and went back to work for Brady as the lead in ALL FOR A GIRL. A miracle—he was a hit in a flop. Then THE CUB and A GENTLEMAN OF LEISURE by P. G. Wodehouse. His contract with Brady expired, and he signed with Cohan and Harris. His final job for them—the lead in OFFICER 666. Then HAWTHORNE OF THE U.S.A.— a success.

Fame at last. Not long afterward, he succumbed to the money of the movies and left for California with his wife and small son.

THE BIRTH OF A NATION had quite suddenly made movies respectable. Douglas was promised Griffith as the director of his first film—but like many Hollywood promises, it vanished in the sun or the klieg lights.

His first film was to be based on one of his Broadway hits—THE NEW HENRIETTA. Changed to BLOOD WILL TELL. Changed to A MAN AND THE TEST. Changed to THE LAMB. Under its final title, it opened, and Douglas Fairbanks was a movie star for good, for the rest of his tragically short life.

In California, he again encountered Mary Pickford. A few more films, and he was the greatest male film star of the day. And Mary the greatest female star.

Did they dare? What would the public say? They dared. The public said Hooray—the hunger for romance was intense, and here they were: America's Sweetheart and the dashingest boy of his time.

Now the story grows faintly dull—more and more success. Richer and richer. More and more celebrated—the world over. Mobs wherever they went, cheering and screaming with love.

With D. W. Griffith and Charlie Chaplin and Samuel Goldwyn, they formed United Artists.

Pickfair—next to the White House, the most famous residence in America. No great celebrity, no member of royalty, no statesman visited California without visiting Pickfair.

It all proved to be too much in the end— the burden of double stardom, the pressures of triumph.

Mary recounts that Doug's standard doodle was a word written, drawn, printed, colored— but always SUCCESS, SUCCESS, SUCCESS.

Remember what Goethe said? "Beware what you wish for in your youth, for you will surely get it in your time."

Douglas Fairbanks got it, and it soured.

A *New York Times* headline on July 3, 1933, read:

"MARY AND DOUG PART"

He married the beautiful Lady Sylvia Ashley, of the international set. She married Buddy Rogers, one of her leading men, who had become a band leader.

Douglas Fairbanks died at fifty-six, worn out.

At her death, in 1979, Mary Pickford was still living at Pickfair—a bitter recluse.

Their films are rarely seen, save in museums. But they did create two worlds of their own—if only it could have been one world.

Douglas Ulman. Toronto. Denver. Gladys Smith.

Pickfair with owners

FRED ASTAIRE and

Marjorie Reynolds

Holiday Inn   1942

Eleanor Powell

Broadway Melody of 1940   1940

Paulette Goddard

Second Chorus   1941

Kay Thompson

Funny Face   1957

Lucille Bremer

Yolanda and the Thief   1945

Betty Hutton

Let's Dance   1950

Nanette Fabray

The Band Wagon   1953

Jane Powell

Royal Wedding   1951

Vera-Ellen

Three Little Words   1951

Joan Leslie

Sky's the Limit   1943

Virginia Dale

Holiday Inn   1942

Rita Hayworth

You'll Never Get Rich   1941

Ann Miller

Easter Parade   1948

Joan Caulfield

Blue Skies   1946

Judy Garland

Easter Parade   1948

Leslie Caron

Daddy Long Legs   1955

Cyd Charisse

The Band Wagon   1953

Audrey Hepburn

Funny Face   1957

Joan Fontaine

Damsel in Distress   1937

Petula Clark

Finian's Rainbow   1968

The Barkleys of Broadway *1949*

They danced for joy. They floated in ecstasy. They leaped for love. They created a style, which is another way of saying "a world of their own"—and we all shared it. They provided matchless entertainment for the eye, complementing perfectly the lovely music they inspired to feed our ears.

The birth of this unique, enchanting TEAM may have been accidental, but its development was not.

Audiences clearly wanted to see more of Astaire and Rogers after their explosive debut in FLYING DOWN TO RIO.

Work began at once on the film version of Fred Astaire's Broadway smash hit, THE GAY DIVORCE, with a thrilling Cole Porter score. It underwent a Breen Office pantywaist title change to THE GAY DIVORCEE. According to the arcane censor's mind, it was moral for a divorcée (female person) to be gay, but not a divorce (institution). And such are the exigencies of our ever-changing, lively American language, that today *neither* of those titles would be acceptable.

The success of THE GAY DIVORCEE, with a smart book by Dwight Taylor and featuring "Night and Day" by Cole Porter, was virtually assured, and disappointed no one.

In the same year, still another Broadway hit was acquired: ROBERTA by Jerome Kern. Then, in astonishing succession, came Irving Berlin's TOP HAT and FOLLOW THE FLEET, Jerome Kern's SWING TIME, and George Gershwin's SHALL WE DANCE.

Here, for reasons never made clear, the TEAM broke up. Had the audiences had enough? Certainly not. Were Astaire and Rogers suffering a kind of marriage fatigue? Possibly. Did they feel artistically drained. Probably. Had they had a personal falling out? Both deny it, although Hollywood gossip stubbornly has it otherwise.

As a matter of relief, the studio brains decided to try a new partner for Fred. They chose Joan Fontaine as his leading lady in DAMSEL IN DISTRESS. Even with the help of an outstanding George and Ira Gershwin score and lyrics, which included "Nice Work If You Can Get It" and "A Foggy Day," plus George

Burns and Gracie Allen in support and George Stevens as director, the picture was a failure.

As the New York *Journal* commented, "The missing link between a smash Astaire hit and just good film fun is Ginger Rogers."

The TEAM was reunited, made Irving Berlin's CAREFREE and THE STORY OF VERNON AND IRENE CASTLE, and broke up again.

Now began a period of Fred Astaire *and* "————". Some of the new partners were patently incompetent. A few were superb. Five were better dancers than Ginger Rogers—but with not a single one of them was there even the suggestion that a TEAM had been formed. The sequence seemed to be one picture, then try a *new* partner. The succession included Joan Fontaine, Eleanor Powell, Paulette Goddard, Rita Hayworth, Marjorie Reynolds, Virginia Dale, Joan Leslie, Lucille Bremer, Joan Caulfield, Ann Miller, Judy Garland, Arlene Dahl, Vera-Ellen, Betty Hutton, Jane Powell, Cyd Charisse, Nanette Fabray, Leslie Caron, Petula Clark, Kay Thompson, and Audrey Hepburn.

Ten years were to pass before Astaire and Rogers were together again—reunited at MGM in THE BARKLEYS OF BROADWAY.

Alas, it had all the tired charm and wilted passion of a warmed-up love affair.

Afterward, both went their separate ways, continuing remarkable and soaring careers—but the magical TEAM was a thing of the past.

Fred Astaire and Ginger Rogers reached the time and place of their meeting by strangely different routes.

He began on May 10, 1899, as Frederick Austerlitz, the son of an officer in Franz Josef's Austro-Hungarian army who had found his way, somehow, to Omaha, Nebraska—and a beautiful local girl named Ann Geilus. I can testify that seventy years later she was still beautiful.

Fred's sister Adele, about a year and a half older, showed early talent for dancing. Her mother put her into the best local school, Chamber's Dancing Academy.

Fred, the sibling, was soon rivaling his sister's leaps and turns and taps.

Mrs. Austerlitz, recognizing the presence of

viable, valuable talent in the family, took off for New York City and Claude Alviènne's famous school.

At five and six respectively, they made a professional debut in Keyport, New Jersey, with new names: Fred and Adele Astaire. ("Astaire" was neither an invention nor a form of Austerlitz—it was actually their grandmother's maiden name.)

Ned Wayburn was their next teacher.

Vaudeville—years of it. Growing up between shows.

Proctor's—with Douglas Fairbanks on the bill.

Before World War I, the Astaires were a highly regarded act and commanded $300 a week on the Orpheum Circuit.

They were still teenagers.

In 1917—Broadway at last. For the Shuberts. The show was OVER THE TOP. Sigmund Romberg score. Ed Wynn in the cast.

THE PASSING SHOW. APPLE BLOSSOMS—score by Fritz Kreisler. THE LOVE LETTER. FOR GOODNESS SAKE. The Astaires were all at once the double toast of the town. THE BUNCH AND JUDY. Then London—made for them. London fell in love with them, and it was reciprocated. STOP FLIRTING ran there for six hundred performances. Gershwin came into their lives. LADY BE GOOD. A smash. Back to London with it. FUNNY FACE. Joined by Marilyn Miller for SMILES produced by Ziegfeld.

About this time Fred was asked to help a new girl named Ginger Rogers with a number in GIRL CRAZY. He did so. It led to a few dates and that was that.

THE BAND WAGON, perhaps the greatest revue in the history of the American theatre.

Adele marries and retires. Fred does THE GAY DIVORCEE and so on and on and on.

Before she was Ginger Rogers, she was Virginia McMath. Born in Independence, Missouri (the Truman town), on July 16, 1911.

A Hollywood try with her mother, Lela. A strikeout. Texas. Lela works on the Fort Worth *Star,* Ginger tries to become a Fort Worth star—dancing, dancing. The Charleston. She excels. It leads to vaudeville—to Chicago

and the Oriental Theater. A marriage to Jack Pepper. Pepper and Ginger.

Broadway: TOP SPEED. A movie! For Paramount, shot on Long Island: YOUNG MAN OF MANHATTAN.

Another show: QUEEN HIGH. Another movie: THE SAP FROM SYRACUSE with Jack Oakie. Then Broadway for GIRL CRAZY. Back to Hollywood and the grind until she had the luck of FLYING DOWN TO RIO.

In the realm of movie TEAMS, Astaire and Rogers are the ultimate. Never before have two personalities been so magically mated.

Each dance they performed was a metaphor for lovemaking.

I recall an evening at Ginger's house when she asked the assembled guests if they would like to see a few Astaire-Rogers numbers. She owned a collection of prints of every number they had ever performed. And so it was that after dinner we all sat down to watch the display. No story, no scenes, simply the numbers, one after another—filled with excitement and charm and sex and beauty and magnetism and erotic dancing. In an hour we were all exhausted as a result of overstimulation. One can watch the act of love performed for only so long.

Yet we rarely saw them kiss. Why not? Fred, when asked to do so, demurred gracefully. "I make love," he said, "with my feet."

It has been suggested that the teaming succeeded because it was not a question of two dancers or two hoofers; rather, it was one superb dancer (Astaire), and one terrific hoofer (Rogers).

Astaire's pre-film career had been confined mainly to dancing. True, he did some singing, but that is not what made him a star. It was a succession of sensational dance routines that he performed with his sister Adele that brought him into the limelight. Later, he performed sketches and proved to be an adept and amiable comedian, but dance was his life and his work.

Ginger Rogers, on the other hand, had built a career based on singing: Gershwin's GIRL CRAZY on Broadway, light comedy in early talkies such as YOUNG MAN OF MANHATTAN in which she said, "Cigarette me, big boy." Later in GOLDDIGGERS OF 1933, and FORTY-SECOND STREET, she sang and danced.

In the teaming with Astaire, she seems infinitely appealing because she is so damned game—trying hard to make it with her suave and elegant and accomplished partner and, by God, she almost always does.

One of the few joys of my being under contract with RKO in the late thirties was being on the lot while Astaire-Rogers pictures were being made. These were the studio's most important productions, and the best of everything was reserved for them.

Months before an Astaire-Rogers went into production, preparations were under way. A great sound stage would be set aside, and for weeks, whenever one walked by, one would see Fred Astaire in dapper rehearsal clothes, sweating it out with Hermes Pan. Early morning, late afternoon, often evening. A pianist and two creative artists digging, discovering, inventing, often astonishing even themselves.

Hermes Pan was a brilliant young Greek dancer and aspiring choreographer from Tennessee whose name was actually Hermes Panagiotopoulos, which he found unwieldy in the world of show business. He had approximately the same build, height, weight, and dimensions as Fred, which made it easy for Fred to work with him on the choreography. The sound stage, while they were rehearsing, was full of blackboards, large and small, detailing the routines in the way that football coaches lay out plays.

After several weeks of preliminary preparation, there would be times when Hermes would be Ginger and Fred Fred and other times Fred would be Ginger and Hermes would be Fred. Finally, Ginger would make her appearance, and the whole process would begin again. Now props were brought in: chairs, sofas, tables. Some weeks of this. Then rehearsals would continue in costume. And hairdress. Each day deepening and enriching the number. After a few months, the director would come in. Usually Mark Sandrich. And the camera ideas would begin. A couple of weeks later, the cameraman would be added to the working team. Finally, shooting would begin.

I once complimented Mark Sandrich on a number he had done, and he replied, "Thank you, but remember—we *ought* to be good by now, we've done so many. And what burns me up sometimes, is realizing how long it took us to learn to shoot an Astaire-Rogers dance. There's one simple principle, and we didn't discover it for years. The principle is never *never* under any circumstances cut away from the dance. In the early pictures, they'd start a dance, and we were so worried that it wouldn't hold, that we'd cut away to people watching. We'd cut away to Eric Blore or Fritz Feld or Helen Broderick doing something—a sight gag, playing a little scene sometimes, to keep the story going. Then we'd cut back to the dance. More and more, we found that we were damaging the number, and still, we didn't seem to have the guts to stay with it. But in the end that proved to be the trick. Never cut away from an Astaire-Rogers number."

The one thing Fred Astaire did not want to be in films was part of a TEAM. He had had a long and successful partnership with his sister Adele, and when she decided to leave the stage and become Lady Cavendish, he was suddenly on his own. The very word "team" offended him. "A team?" he once said. "It sounds like a pair of horses!"

Adele claims she had grown tired of the difficult life she had led for so many years, was stuck on Charlie, but that nothing seemed to be happening to solidify the relationship.

One night, at "21," which was still a speakeasy, she and Cavendish were having supper. They ordered a drink. She was a teetotaler, but when she finished the drink, she was all at once emboldened and said, "Listen, Charlie, we like each other, and we get along. Why don't we get married?"

"All right," he said.

And they went on with their supper. She says that the following morning, he called her and reminded her of the proposal. She remembered it, but fuzzily. However, it was done.

The team of Fred and Adele Astaire—*a rara avis*—was finished.

A trouper to the last, she agreed to stay with

the show they were doing, THE BAND WAGON, until the end of its New York run. It turned out that even then it was not possible for her to leave because no replacement had been found. She went on tour with the show to Chicago. Early in March 1932, a replacement was found in the person of Vera Marsh. Adele Astaire walked out of the stage door of the Illinois Theatre in Chicago, ending her career.

Fred, after all the years of dancing with Adele, found it almost impossible to function with Vera Marsh, although she was an accomplished dancer and a charming personality.

The months that followed were so difficult that he determined never to be part of a team again. He was his own man now, he would make it on his own.

By and large, careers defy design and planning. There are too many imponderables involved. Too many accidents and happenstances. A certain property turns up at a given moment, someone dies, someone is replaced, a writer creates a character or a set of characters and the best-laid schemes *gang aft agley*.

So it was for Fred Astaire who, much against his will and design and scheme, found himself part of one of the most successful TEAMS the screen has ever known.

The circumstances became increasingly irresistible. RKO began to provide the best composers: Cole Porter, Jerome Kern, Irving Berlin, George Gershwin, Vincent Youmans; the finest directors, designers, cameramen, arrangers. As a result, the Astaire-Rogers pictures had that most ineffable quality, *class*. How beautifully they played together, sang together, danced together, existed together. And how strange that this romantic ideal of a partnership should have been confined to shadows on the screen. In their off-screen life, they were scarcely compatible. They liked each other, respected each other, and worked without friction of any kind, but when the day's work was over, they were strangers. They shared no social life whatever. It has been said that Fred Astaire never saw the inside of Ginger's house, nor she of his. Yet both were gregarious people who entertained constantly.

They lived in different worlds in the Hollywood system of cliques and claques.

The world they created and shared with their vast audience was unforgettable. Whenever an Astaire-Rogers film plays and I can get to it, I do. The magic, the wonder, the appeal is always there still. It is not simply a matter of sentiment and nostalgia. It is a matter of being in the presence of perfection. Their talents shine luminously. They are Utopians.

I always leave the theatre feeling better than I did when I went in.

In their first seven pictures, all of them romantic, Ginger remains kissless. Some thought it was a question of Fred Astaire's wife, Phyllis, who it was thought might not take kindly to the idea. Fred laughed at this notion and said it was only to avoid the same sort of mush the audiences saw in practically every other picture. There were other speculations as well, but no one knows, not even now.

Audiences began to wonder about this kissless romance. And a fan magazine ran a story called "Why Won't Fred Kiss Ginger???"

Finally, in CAREFREE, their first color film, it happened. Irving Berlin had written the score, including a number called "I Used to Be Color Blind." The dance performed to this number was a slow-motion sequence and the kiss was the climax.

In CAREFREE there was also a number that again demonstrated Astaire's search for perfection through precision. It was "Since They Turned Loch Lomond into Swing," and Fred, an expert golfer, did a dance built around golf swings. No one who saw it is likely to forget it. It took two weeks to shoot, during which he lost seven hundred golf balls.

The Astaire-Rogers partnership often resembled a troubled marriage. He had not wanted to be part of a TEAM from the beginning. And as he and Ginger made one successful picture after another, he saw himself being trapped into this relationship.

Ginger was somewhat more fortunate. Between the Astaire-Rogers outputs, she managed to make other pictures that went well.

So, from time to time, when one or both of them felt they wanted to end the partnership,

Shall We Dance   *1937*

Top Hat *1935*

there would be a long period of time without an Astaire-Rogers, but during this period, the front office was continually plotting ways to get them back together again. Not for reasons of sentiment, but of cash. It must be remembered that films were still using the block-booking system, which meant that an Astaire-Rogers offered to the exhibitors sometimes meant that five or six or seven other pictures could be sold along with it automatically. Sometimes even more. Sometimes the whole program.

Even after FLYING DOWN TO RIO and THE GAY DIVORCEE, Astaire-Rogers were still not considered stars, so when ROBERTA was being planned, Irene Dunne, who *was* a star, was cast to protect the marquee value of the project.

ROBERTA had been no great shakes on the stage and had its mild success mainly as the result of a single smash hit song, "Smoke Gets in Your Eyes."

Max Gordon, the producer of ROBERTA in the theatre, recounts that in 1936 when his great chum Noel Coward arrived from England on the *Queen Mary,* he came directly from the pier to the New Amsterdam Theatre to see a matinee of ROBERTA. When the show was over, Max was waiting for him at the back of the house. Coward came floating up the aisle, saw Max, embraced him heartily, and shouted, *"Max, darling! It stinks!"*

The movie was an improvement. Still the only thing that seemed to matter was the fantastic TEAM of Astaire and Rogers doing what had never been done before on the screen. The score was beefed up. "Smoke Gets in Your Eyes" was left in, "I Won't Dance" and "Lovely to Look At" by Dorothy Fields and Jimmy Mc-Hugh were added.

The outstanding number was "I'll Be Hard to Handle."

Following this remarkable routine there was nothing Astaire or Rogers or the studio could do to keep them from exploding.

Writing about the picture, the *New York Times* said, "The Kublai Khans and RKO have directed a bright and shimmering pleasure dome. The work is a model of urbanity in the musical films, and Mr. Astaire, the debonair master of light comedy and the dance, is its chief ornament.

"To watch him skipping on effortless cat's feet across a dance floor is to experience one of the major delights of the contemporary cinema. The only fault in the production is that Mr. Astaire and his excellent partner, Miss Rogers, cannot be dancing during every minute of it."

There was nothing to do now but plan a new picture. And what a picture it turned out to be! Irving Berlin was engaged to do the score, and since he was a songwriter who always wrote precisely for the talents of whichever star he was working with, "Top Hat, White Tie, and Tails" came to his mind at once. For the first TEAM number he came up with "Cheek to Cheek" and then, "Isn't This a Lovely Day?" Finally, a spectacular novelty dance called "The Piccolino."

I remember going to see TOP HAT at the Radio City Music Hall on its opening day. Never before and never since have I seen an audience stand up and cheer at the end of a picture. A standing ovation for a movie? I sat through the picture twice and that evening insisted on going again and taking my brother with me. Twice for him too, which meant four times that day for me. The next evening I was back again. Only once through this time. Then I went back every single evening, each time taking a beloved friend and enjoying it anew through his or her eyes.

TOP HAT was, unquestionably, a breakthrough, a milestone. The musical screen was growing up. This was a brand of sophistication new, not only to it, but to most of the musical shows on Broadway.

The unprecedented success of TOP HAT gave the studio the idea that they should not tamper with the setup. Irving Berlin was engaged again. Mark Sandrich was signed. Work began on FOLLOW THE FLEET. It was actually the old Broadway success HIT THE DECK, which had been adapted from a silent called SHORE-LEAVE, done in 1925.

Again, Berlin happily writing for his pal Fred, came up with one of his most inventive scores. Fred was a sailor, Ginger a dime-a-dance girl. Berlin wrote "We Saw the Sea" as well as "I'm Putting All My Eggs in One Basket," then "Let's Face the Music and Dance."

A row between the studio and the TEAM over salary held up production of the next picture, SWING TIME. This had a score by Jerome Kern. It was thought that a new director might keep the TEAM from going stale. George Stevens was engaged.

Fred got into blackface and did a remarkable number called "Bojangles of Harlem" as a tribute to the great Bill Robinson. The other numbers were top drawer Kern with lyrics by Dorothy Fields: "A Fine Romance" and "The Way You Look Tonight."

For the next picture Mark Sandrich was brought back. The picture was called SHALL WE DANCE and had a score by the Gershwins that is as good as anything they ever did. "They All Laughed," "Let's Call the Whole Thing Off," "They Can't Take That Away From Me," "Slap That Bass," and "Beginner's Luck." All these in addition to the title song.

The picture also had in it one of the most daring dance numbers ever. A number performed on roller skates. It took a month to prepare, four and a half days to shoot, and was on the screen for less than three minutes. The dangers inherent were enormous. But the TEAM took a chance and triumphed.

In the finale, the audience was astonished to see Fred Astaire dancing, not with Ginger, but with the well-known ballerina Harriet Hoctor. That was the way of gently breaking the news to the public that Astaire and Rogers were no longer going to make pictures together.

Blue Skies   *1946*

Rebecca   1940

Anna Karenina   1948

LAURENCE OLIVIER and VIVIEN LEIGH

Individually, they were real as real can be.

He, a master of pragmatism—an iconoclast where film or theatre nonsense is concerned. A worker, a rehearser, a perfectionist. A typical statement: "I'd rather run the scene eight times than waste time chattering about abstractions. An actor gets the thing right by doing it over and over. Arguing about motivations and so forth is a lot of rot."

Unlike most great actors, he is equally gifted as a director; and unlike most directors, is a commanding executive—as witness his twelve-year tenure as managing director of Britain's National Theatre, a post he filled magnificently while acting in and directing many of its outstanding productions. Real.

She, a stunner whose ravishing beauty often tended to obscure her staggering achievements as an actress. Great beauties are infrequently great actresses—simply because they do not need to be. Vivien was different; ambitious, persevering, serious, often inspired. She did not use her beauty, she presented other gifts: a perfect housekeeper, knowledgeable about food and wine and napery and china and silver and bedmaking and cheese. Having been born in India and educated largely in European schools, she was mellifluously fluent in French and knew German and Italian, as well. She was deep into music and world literature and held acutely personal judgments and opinions. Wildly witty, too. All in all, a smashing girl. And real.

"I'm certain," she once said, "that it is good for one to have some enthusiasm in life right away from one's profession. Mine happens to be the good earth. I love gardening, weeding, planting, flowers."

Together, however, as a TEAM, Olivier and Leigh were anything *but* real. They presented the ultimate romantic vision. A Heaven-made match. To see them together in life or on the screen or stage was a heady experience. They seemed to leave the real world and to exist an inch off the ground.

Vivien Leigh and Laurence Olivier met on a film called FIRE OVER ENGLAND. Vivien played a lady-in-waiting to Queen Elizabeth (Flora Robson). The best part of Larry's role was its name: Michael Ingoldsby. Others in the cast were Leslie Banks, Robert Newton, and Raymond Massey.

Larry's scenes called for a number of daredevil stunts. He insisted upon doing them himself, although William K. Howard, the director, argued for a stuntman. Larry prevailed. It has been suggested that his confessed admiration for Douglas Fairbanks may have been involved. Another fair guess is that he was showing off for Vivien in the manner of a reckless schoolboy or a successful peacock.

No one who saw them in this film could doubt that they were ordained to be an acting TEAM. Their very first scene together created magic—powerful and dizzying. She was twenty-two and a rising young player. He was already, at thirty, one of the outstanding British actors whose future was assured.

Both were married; she to Leigh Holman, a barrister, he to Jill Esmond, an actress with whom he often appeared—notably with Noel Coward and Gertrude Lawrence in the Broadway production of PRIVATE LIVES.

Movie-set romances are not uncommon—in fact, they are often inevitable, but usually end with the last day of shooting.

Not so for Olivier and Leigh. On the last day, they exchanged gifts. He gave her an exquisite cameo; she gave him a large, satchel-like leather briefcase. Twenty years later, he was still using it, and it had acquired a name.

"Put this into *Fire over England*, love, would you?"

"Oh, hell! I can't find *Fire over England!*"

"Don't forget *Fire over England*, darling."

That same year, they made another movie, 21 DAYS. (U.S. release title: 21 DAYS TOGETHER.) So undistinguished and inferior is this silly melodrama that one is led to suspect that Olivier and Leigh did it only in order to be together. The plot: the ne'er-do-well brother of an eminent barrister accidentally kills the husband of his mistress. An innocent man is accused of the crime and is remanded for twenty-one days. The ne'er-do-well spends this time with his mistress prior to giving himself

That Hamilton Woman   *1941*

21 Days Together   *1940*

Fire over England   *1937*

On another occasion, he said something that may be a clue to the agony that lay ahead in darker days: "It is unfortunate that Vivien's and my conversations, which should be normal conversations, are all too frequently conferences about some business problem or some theatre problem."

After THAT HAMILTON WOMAN, they were never to make another film together. Both went on to soaring stardom, but there were constant obstacles to their teaming: her long-term contract with David O. Selznick; World War II; Laurence Olivier in the Royal Navy; making HENRY V; his work in saving the Old Vic, managing and playing; the difficulty in finding vehicles.

We once planned a production of THE ADMIRABLE CRICHTON for Korda, but again, it was not to be.

Vivien once said: "Among more particular and personal regrets and disappointments, I confess that I should dearly liked to have played with my husband in the films of *Wuthering Heights* and *Rebecca*. They gave me abundant tests for the heroine in the latter film in Hollywood, then came to the conclusion that I looked 'foxy.' An epithet with which I quite wildly disagree! Foxy, indeed!"

It is difficult for me to imagine anyone turning Vivien down for anything.

The TEAM lived triumphantly, however, in the theatre.

Their joint production of ANTONY AND CLEOPATRA by Shakespeare, in conjunction with CAESAR AND CLEOPATRA by Shaw, was an inspired, daring project, as overwhelming in execution as in concept.

A great MACBETH at Stratford-upon-Avon. They made every possible attempt to film this but were met by rejection on all fronts. As a friend, I tried in every way I knew to get them backing—the cold business answer was no. They offered to work gratis. Still no takers. Thus a filmed MACBETH with Laurence Olivier and Vivien Leigh, which might have existed, does not.

They made a world tour with the Old Vic, playing THE SCHOOL FOR SCANDAL, THE SKIN OF OUR TEETH, and RICHARD III.

Later, they had one of their most glittering successes with THE SLEEPING PRINCE by Terence Rattigan. But when the movie version came to be made, it was Marilyn Monroe instead of Vivien Leigh—and the title was changed sleazily to THE PRINCE AND THE SHOWGIRL.

Small wonder that Vivien's always frail health was adversely affected.

The pressures and strains of professional and personal life finally proved too much in 1958—and the TEAM was no more.

When I heard the news, I could think only of a star-filled August sky above Santa Barbara, California, under which, on a ranch patio, a merry wedding was in progress. Vivien, the bride; Larry, the groom; I, the best man. Kate Hepburn, a witness. A tipsy justice of the peace, who conducted a mumbled, jumbled ceremony, ending with a cry of "Bingo!"

A marriage hand-made in Heaven had been consummated, at last, on earth. What could possibly go wrong, ever? Nothing. Perfection is permanent.

Laurence Olivier went on to ever-increasing triumph. Vivien Leigh continued a career of sorts, but it was easy to see that her heart was not in her work—it had remained behind, still part of the glorious Olivier-Leigh TEAM.

On July 8, 1967, Vivien died—suddenly, unexpectedly, uselessly. Had she not done so, we might have seen this wondrous TEAM again, for Vivien and Larry remained friends even after the failure of their marriage.

As it is, we must be content with the shining memory of the glamour and beauty and romance and magic they brought onto the screen and into our lives.

Fire over England *1937*

Pillow Talk   *1959*

Pillow Talk *1959*

ROCK HUDSON and DORIS DAY

These days, it is fashionable to look at the Rock Hudson-Doris Day pictures as something in the nature of high camp, subject to easy ridicule since they bear little relationship to life. Moreover, they have the disadvantage to some eyes of having been overwhelmingly successful box office hits.

The fact is that, in their day, they were intelligently crafted, sophisticatedly conceived, and brilliantly produced. Their principal asset, however, was not Doris Day, not Rock Hudson, but Rock Hudson and Doris Day.

Doris Day was born Doris von Kappelhoff (why did she ever change it?) on April 4, 1924, in Cincinnati, Ohio. And no matter what happened to her in the years that followed, whether she was a successful amateur contestant, a small-time band singer, a big-time band singer, a starlet, a movie star, a superstar—she remained, indubitably, a girl from Cincinnati, Ohio.

Roy Fitzgerald, Jr., who was to become Rock Hudson, was born in Winnetka, Illinois, on November 17, 1927. He is an extremely tall —6 feet 4 inches—unquestionably attractive, typical movie leading man.

Hudson and Day went into films at precisely the same time, 1948—but it was to be ten years before they became a TEAM.

Rock Hudson. One can almost conjure up the conference at which the name was created. Numerology doubtless came into play; subliminal images; psychology of various sorts.

"Hudson's good. Strong. Fits."

"Ralph Hudson?"

"Ross Hudson!"

"Rick Hudson?"

"Ron Hudson!"

"Rod Hudson?"

"Hey, how about Rock?"

"That's a name? Rock?"

"Sure, why not?"

"Rock Hudson?"

"He *looks* like a rock, doesn't he?"

"You mean he *acts* like a rock."

"All right, never mind that."

"So what's it going to be?"

"Rod Hudson?"

"No, Rock."

"Not bad."

"Rock Hudson."

He began at Warner Brothers in FIGHTER SQUADRON and went on playing small parts in big pictures and big parts in small pictures. In his first ten years, he made thirty-eight. Among them: I WAS A SHOPLIFTER, THE FAT MAN (someone must have heard of THE THIN MAN), TOMAHAWK, IRON MAN, HERE COME THE NELSONS, THE LAWLESS BREED, SEMINOLE, TAZA, SON OF COCHISE, CAPTAIN LIGHTFOOT, FOUR GIRLS IN TOWN, and TWILIGHT FOR THE GODS.

His best part was the so-called lead opposite Elizabeth Taylor in GIANT, where he was completely overshadowed by Elizabeth Taylor, James Dean, and the production itself.

In 1959, Doris Day, whose career had been somewhat more impressive, was beginning to fade. She had scored solid successes, mainly in LOVE ME OR LEAVE ME, THE PAJAMA GAME, and TEACHER'S PET opposite Clark Gable. Then came two disasters: THE TUNNEL OF LOVE and IT HAPPENED TO JANE. Something had to be done.

Her husband, Martin Melcher, a skillful promoter, decided that what she needed was a teammate.

It was Ross Hunter's idea to team her with Rock Hudson, although Martin Melcher generally took credit for the idea.

Rock Hudson's first contact with Doris Day came in 1944. He was in the Navy, being shipped out from San Francisco on a troopship to an unknown destination. The night the troopship sailed, it passed under the Golden Gate Bridge, its lights went on, and the voice of Doris Day singing "Sentimental Journey" came on over the loudspeaker. He later recalled that the whole ship was in tears, including himself.

Fifteen years were to pass before he met the owner of the voice.

Roy Fitzgerald's career in the United States Navy, which he joined as soon as he was graduated from high school, was undistinguished. It was a wartime navy, and even though he began as an aviation mechanic, he finished as a laundryman third-class. Hardly a case of the climb up the naval ladder.

When he was demobilized, he went to Los Angeles to look for a job. He became a vacuum cleaner salesman, then a truck driver, and finally, a mailman. One of the people on his route was the celebrated Hollywood agent, Henry Willson, who was not only the discoverer but clearly the namer of such screen personalities as Tab Hunter, Guy Madison, Rory Calhoun, and Race Gentry. Willson, an affable chap, became friends with his mailman, and asked him one day if he had ever acted. Roy replied that he had acted in school plays. This was enough for Willson, who arranged a test for him at Twentieth Century-Fox, which did not turn out well at all. Willson then took him to Raoul Walsh, who was about to make FIGHTER SQUADRON at Warner's. And largely as a favor to Willson, Walsh gave him a bit.

He looked good on screen, and Warner's offered him a stock contract. Roy turned it down, and instead, signed a contract with Walsh and Willson at $125 a week, which was a little less than he had been earning as a mailman.

About a year later, Willson and Walsh sold the contract to Universal, and Rock Hudson's career was underway.

Hudson on the subject of his early films:

"Most of them make me cringe. It's rather like having your old linen washed in public, but at least those lousy movies were good training. The only thing I can say in my defense is that I did the best I could. It was pretty rotten, I agree, but it was my best. . . . Oddly enough, my greatest worry in those days was that I'd muff a line and waste film."

One of the conditions of the Rock Hudson-Doris Day deal was that Martin Melcher be engaged as coproducer. His first idea was to change the title of PILLOW TALK to THE WAY THE WIND BLOWS. Coincidentally, this was the title of a song Melcher was about to publish. He dabbled in song publishing as a sideline, and apparently had as many sidelines as he had ideas. The picture, in the end, of course, was called PILLOW TALK. Good title. They engaged Tony Randall as the third lead. Good choice. Thelma Ritter as the character relief. Marvel-

ous idea. From then on, all went smoothly, and it was clear that the TEAM was going to be around for a long time.

When they made PILLOW TALK, Doris Day was thirty-five years old, and Rock Hudson thirty-two.

It is something of a triumph of her acting ability that this disparity was never noticed.

Doris Day says, "I had never met Rock Hudson before, but the very first day on the set, I discovered we had a performing rapport that was remarkable. We played our scenes together as if we had once lived them."

The picture itself was a solid success with the critics and with the public. Even so knowledgeable a reviewer as Arthur Knight in the *Saturday Review* called it "the year's most sophisticated light comedy. . . . It's one occasion where everyone concerned seems to know exactly what he is doing and does it well." Virtually all the reviews were in the same vein.

Marty Melcher ascribed the success of the picture to "clean sex comedy, enticing but legal —a good formula."

In her ten-year career, Doris Day had never been nominated for an Academy Award, and for PILLOW TALK she was, but lost to Simone Signoret for ROOM AT THE TOP. The original screenplay by Russell Rouse, Clarence Greene, and Stanley Shapiro did win the Academy Award.

Following PILLOW TALK, Doris Day became the number one motion-picture box-office star. And such is the momentum of popular acceptance that she remained the number one star for five years.

It took nearly two years to prepare the second picture for the TEAM, LOVER COME BACK.

If anything, this was even more successful than the first. Bosley Crowther, in the *New York Times,* wrote: "Mr. Hudson and Miss Day are delicious, he in his big sprawling way, and she in her wide-eyed, pert, pugnacious, and eventually melting vein."

According to A. E. Hotchner, here is Rock Hudson on the subject of TEAMS:

"I don't really know what makes a movie

Send Me No Flowers   *1964*

Pillow Talk *1959*

Send Me No Flowers   *1964*

Send Me No Flowers   *1964*

Send Me No Flowers   *1964*

Pillow Talk   *1959*

team. Gable and Lombard. Tracy and Hepburn. I recently saw an old flick starring Joan Crawford and Spencer Tracy in a 'team' picture, and that was a glaring example of what didn't work. Absolutely no chemistry between them. But when Tracy teamed with Hepburn, it worked like a charm. I'd say, first of all, the two people have to truly like each other, as Doris and I did, for that shines through, the sparkle, the twinkle in the eye as the two people look at each other. Then, too, both parties have to be strong personalities—very important to comedy so that there's a tug-of-war over who's going to put it over on the other, who's going to get the last word, a fencing match between adroit opponents of the opposite sex who in the end are going to fall in bed together.''

Martin Melcher became obsessively irritated at the praise being garnered by the Rock Hudson–Doris Day TEAM. In an attempt to show that she did not need a teammate but rather a leading man, he dropped Hudson in the next picture which had been prepared for the TEAM and substituted Cary Grant.

No sensible film observer is going to deny that Cary Grant is a far more accomplished farceur than Rock Hudson. Why then was THAT TOUCH OF MINK such a dismal failure? We are back to the mystery of teaming. Rock Hudson and Doris Day worked. Cary Grant and Doris Day did not.

And so in the next picture, Rock Hudson was back.

It was their third—SEND ME NO FLOWERS. This was successful enough with the public, who had taken to the TEAM, but less so with the critics.

Still, the fact that it grossed something less than LOVER COME BACK convinced the hard-nosed Melcher that something had to be done. Obviously, it could not be the fault of Doris or of the picture he had so carefully worked out. It had to be Rock Hudson. So Hudson was dropped from the TEAM and a new partner was found for Doris Day in the person of Rod Taylor (real name Rock Taylor?)

Their first movie together was DO NOT DISTURB. Well unremembered. Then THE GLASS BOTTOM BOAT, another catastrophe. It was de-

cided that Rod Taylor simply would not do.

What to do? Try Rock Hudson with her again? It was considered, of course, but on the basis of their last failure, the powers decreed that the TEAM was through.

Doris Day went on to CAPRICE and THE BALLAD OF JOSIE, and virtually ended her film career. Similarly, Rock Hudson's search for a hit failed.

The basic mistake that was made in the handling of the Doris Day image was that she was asked to play the same age for a decade. Not only the same age, but the same undeveloped, undeveloping person.

Later, both dived opportunistically into the burgeoning television business, she with THE DORIS DAY SHOW, he with MACMILLAN AND WIFE. Both were reasonably successful, but neither he nor she ever achieved again the charm or personality or interplay or magnetism they created when they played so beautifully together.

Send Me No Flowers   *1964*

CRAZY TEAMS

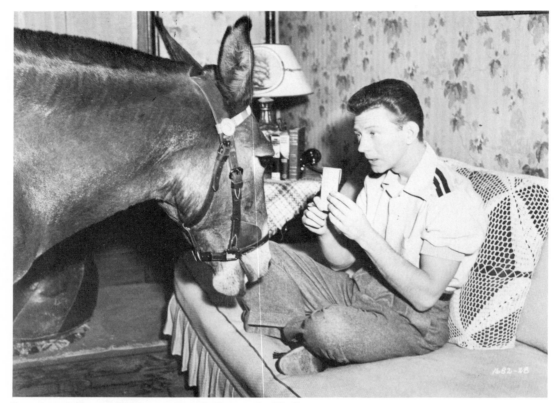

Francis and Donald O'Connor   Francis Covers the Big Town   *1953*

Boris Karloff and Bela Lugosi   The Raven   *1935*

W. C. Fields and Mae West   My Little Chickadee   *1940*

Bill Robinson and Shirley Temple   The Little Colonel   *1935*

Marriage Italian Style *1964*

The Latin Lovers
SOPHIA LOREN and MARCELLO MASTROIANNI

Stendhal once wrote: "The French exist in a false relationship to love. Go to Italy! Go to Italy, where love is *total.*"

This precept is passionately exemplified in the vibes created by the relationship of Sophia Loren and Marcello Mastroianni on screen. Total, indeed.

Italian men are interested in women. Moreover, they let the women know it. Marcello Mastroianni, discussing Sophia Loren, says: "She has a femininity, a maternal sense that is ancient in women, but rare to find today. She has a force one can find in one's own mother, a moral strength that in a short while will no longer exist. I've taken her to my mother's home many times. She's the only actress I've been tied to out of affection for more than ten years. In the movie world, that's quite a long time."

Sophia Loren was born in Rome in 1934, the illegitimate daughter of Romilda Villani, a Naples girl, and Riccardo Scicolone, a good-looking construction engineer. She grew up in the suburbs of Naples with her grandmother and a younger sister, Maria. The gallant Riccardo finally married another woman, and his two daughters were left to roam the streets.

As a little girl, Sophia was known as Stechetto (Toothpick), but in time outgrew that appellation.

She recalls: "The first movie I saw at the age of four was an American film of *The Picture of Dorian Gray* with Hurd Hatfield, Angela Lansbury, and George Sanders. Next I saw a film with Yvonne DeCarlo, whom I adored. After I saw Tyrone Power in *The Mark of Zorro,* I went back to see it over and over again. I would go the first thing in the morning and stay through the last showing at night. There was always something magic to me about movies. I couldn't get over the way it was: on the walls, persons suddenly started to live. For years I always used to look where the projector was to see where the people came from."

From that time on, she haunted the movie houses—sneaking in when necessary—to watch Astaire and Rogers, Betty Grable, Judy Gar-land ("about a rainbow"), and Gene Kelly.

"Like every little girl in every little Italian town," she recalls, "the movies were our only pleasure. They gave us dreams about a life we didn't have."

At the age of fourteen, she entered a beauty contest for the selection of "Queen of the Sea of Naples" and her court. There were 320 contestants. Sophia won second place and thus became one of the princesses. She used the prize money to go to Rome with her mother.

This formidable woman, who had once won a Greta Garbo look-alike contest, had long nurtured dreams of becoming an actress. When she heard that an American production of QUO VADIS was being made at Cinécittà, she made her way there with Sophia. They applied for positions as extras, were hired, and worked for one night, for which they were paid $32.

A Hollywood game used to be that of trying to spot Sophia in the picture. Sharp eyes recognized her as one of the slaves fanning Deborah Kerr.

In 1950, Sophia entered yet another beauty contest for the selection of Miss Rome, but lost. (Who do you suppose *won?*) Her good fortune, however, was that Carlo Ponti, a successful film producer, was one of the judges. He got her a screen test, but she failed it badly. Her hair was too short, and she was still extremely thin. Ponti told her to give up any thought of becoming a film actress because she did not photograph well.

She turned to modeling and became fairly well-known in the field. This, in time, led to a few movie bits, then to the lead in the film AIDA, for which Renata Tebaldi did the singing. Seeing her in this, Carlo Ponti apparently changed his mind. (What happened is simple to explain. The war-starved adolescent's skin and bones made her difficult to photograph. When she fleshed out—and with *what* flesh!—she became a classic beauty. There are, one observes, advantages in being well-fed.) Ponti offered her not only a four-year film contract, but a lifetime contract as his wife. They were married in September 1957 in Mexico, and her real film career was under way.

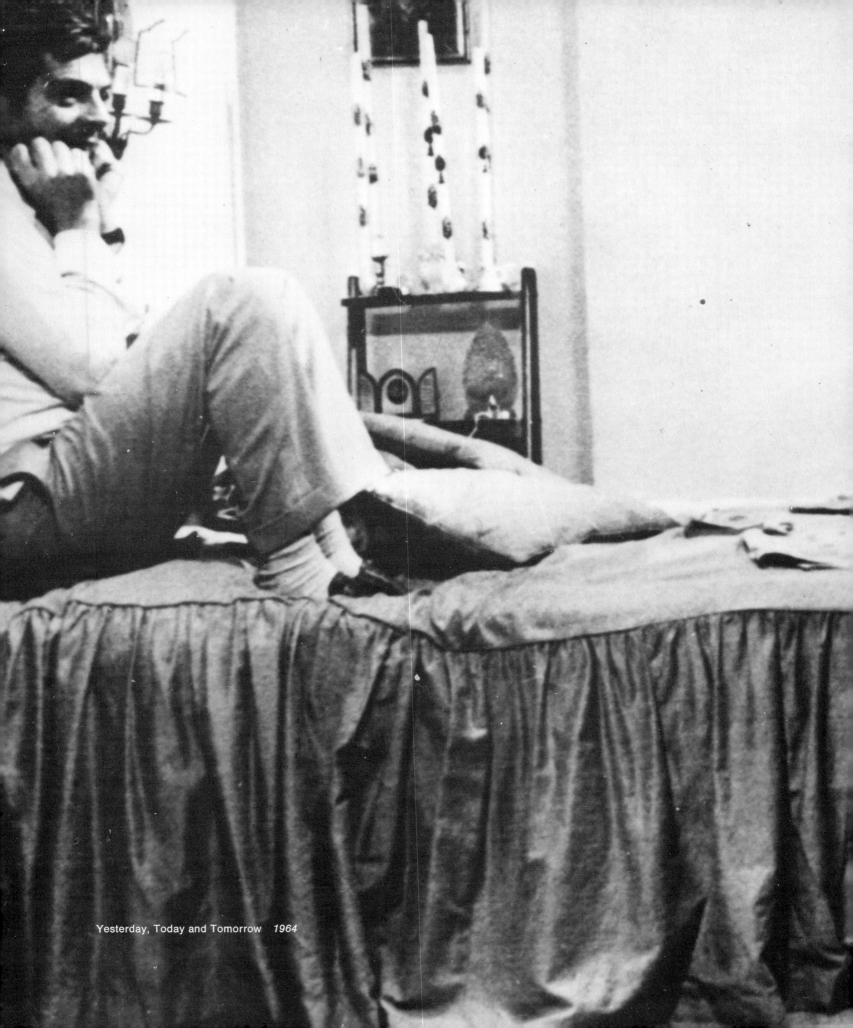

Yesterday, Today and Tomorrow   1964

Sunflower   *1970*

Yesterday, Today and Tomorrow   *1964*

Marriage Italian Style   *1964*

The Miller's Beautiful Wife   *1955*

She was asked to change her name. Sophia Scicolone was thought to be unwieldy. A press agent, playing around with ideas, happened to be fond of the actress Marta Toren. He experimented with variations on that "Toren," coming up with "Boren," "Doren," "Moren," and finally hit on "Loren."

Sophia Loren developed into one of the finest film actresses of her time and gave some of the most memorable and lasting screen performances we are likely to see.

It is true that not a single one of her Hollywood films succeeded, but this is the fault of Hollywood, not of Sophia Loren. In Hollywood, she was misunderstood, mistreated, and mishandled. A great opportunity was missed.

She herself has few regrets about that Hollywood period, regarding it as a kind of training school which additionally made her into a bankable name, so that in time she was able to get the lead in De Sica's TWO WOMEN, for which she won an Academy Award.

Sophia Loren has made over seventy-five films since her career began in 1959; almost four films a year, considering that there were long periods when she left the screen to attempt to have children. This became an obsession with her. After two miscarriages, it was necessary for her to confine herself to hospitals for long periods of time in order to realize her dream, which eventually she did, producing two fine sons—Carlo Junior ("Cipi") and Eduardo ("Eli").

Marcello Mastroianni was born in the village of Fontana Liri, south of Rome, on September 28, 1923. His early education was in graphic art, and during World War II, he became an industrial designer.

Following the Italian armistice, he was imprisoned by the Germans. With a friend, he escaped and managed somehow to reach Venice.

When the war ended, he went to work as an accountant in the offices of the British film company, Eagle Lion, and as a lark, joined a theatrical company called the University Players in Rome.

His gifts as an actor were almost immediately recognized, and in 1948 he was cast in a professional stage production of a play called ANGELICA, with Giulietta Masina.

In 1951, he starred in the Italian production of A STREETCAR NAMED DESIRE and scored an outstanding success. This was followed by a second success in Arthur Miller's DEATH OF A SALESMAN.

Before long, he was one of the greatest stars of the Italian cinema, doubtless because he had the great good fortune of playing his first important parts opposite Sophia Loren in LA BELLA MUGNAIA and LA FORTUNA DI ESSERE DONNA.

In 1959 came Fellini's LA DOLCE VITA, and Marcello Mastroianni became a worldwide film star. He worked under the direction of Fellini, Visconti, Antonioni, De Sica, and every other important film director in Italy. He is still perhaps the most in-demand film actor in the world. He has made any number of distinguished films, many of them released in the United States, such as LA NOTTE, THE ORGANIZER, A VERY PRIVATE AFFAIR, FAMILY DIARY, Fellini's great 8½, De Sica's YESTERDAY, TODAY AND TOMORROW, De Sica's MARRIAGE ITALIAN STYLE, Monicelli's CASANOVA 70; but the most popular of his films are the ones he has made with his adored Sophia. In 1978, A SPECIAL DAY.

It seems clear that no TEAM is interesting unless the participants are evenly matched. No one wants to see a tennis match between Jimmy Connors and Art Buchwald. Prizefights are only good when the match is even. In business, in marriage, in a partnership of any kind, an equal balance is the element that makes for success.

One of the difficulties of providing leading men for Sophia Loren is the fact that she is so strong, so arresting, so dominating, so ballsy a personality, that most mere actors are wiped off the screen by her presence.

Even Cary Grant was barely able to hold his own against her, and when she was matched with such players as Tab Hunter, Steve Forrest or Tony Perkins, the results were ludicrous.

In Marcello Mastroianni, she finds her match. Strong as she is, he returns the favor brilliantly.

Yet it must be observed that at no time

does Sophia lose one whit of her magnetic femininity.

It has been said that William Shakespeare's genius in creating characters is that he makes his most ineffably feminine women strong at times as men, and that he makes his most powerful men often soft as women. Consider Portia and Juliet, Lady Macbeth, Beatrice, and Rosalind. Conversely: Othello, Hamlet, Richard III, King Lear.

Similarly, the personae of both Mastroianni and Loren follow this rule. Manly and authoritative and powerful as he is, we are not surprised to see him collapse into tenderness or cry bitter tears of frustration and weakness. On the other hand, utterly female and desirable and alluring as she is, we believe it when Sophia takes charge and cracks the whip.

When someone suggested to Mastroianni that he was the Clark Gable of the present, he scoffed, "If anything, I'm the anti-Gable. He was the type of hero who was popular yesterday. Gable and others like Gary Cooper played strong, clean men, full of virtue and honesty. They were decisive and solid and knew where they were going. Or they lived in a world which presumed that a he-man always knew where he was going. But today we *don't* know where we're going. . . . In my roles, I reveal that I am simply human. This confession of the human condition is the difference between myself and Gable. In this sense I play myself. He played a myth, a myth that was credible yesterday but I think not today. If Gable were to begin again with the same image, I doubt he would become King Gable."

And the following statement by Sophia makes one see why she and Mastroianni were always and always will be so compatible:

"I am an actress who has to identify myself with a role or I can't play it. What I like is a role with everything all together, not just in one direction like violence or eroticism. I like to play people who are fundamentally very human. It's impossible for me to play a role I don't feel. The woman you see on the screen is me."

Some years ago, the distinguished writer John Cheever did an interview with Sophia.

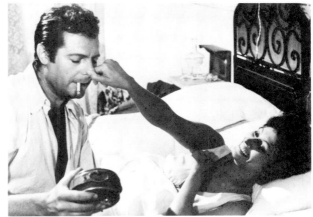
Sunflower *1970*

A Special Day *1977*

Yesterday, Today and Tomorrow *1964*

Yesterday, Today and Tomorrow *1964*

The Millionairess 1961

Blowout   *1973*

She respected him so much more than an ordinary journalist that she spoke freely and easily.

"What do I like? I like thunderstorms. I love thunder and lightning. Waterfalls depress me. I like all kinds of smells. I like the smell of the sea and I like Patou's Joy. And I love the smell of stables, I think because it reminds me of the milk my mother got for me during the war. It kept me alive. I like bright colors. They all have meaning for me. Red is the color of courage and love. Black is the color of pain. I think of names as colors. Loren is orange. Ponti is blue. . . . I would like a good part in a play, but they are hard to find. . . . A play would be very different from films, of course, but it must be exciting to have a new audience every night. I would like to do tragedy. This might be for me a death leap, but I know about tragedy and I would like to try. I like a performance to have the sense of giving something. I am also frightened and I am never confident that I have been successful. I like to sing. This frightens me because I am a perfectionist and I know my voice is limited. But I could not live without singing. I sang a song in a television show, and some critic said that I was no Barbra Streisand, but when I met Barbra in London, she told me not to worry. She said that if she looked like me, she wouldn't bother to speak. . . . So those are some of the things that I like. What I don't like is harder. I don't like tranquilizers. I don't like pep pills. I don't like tape recorders. I always say *something* that shouldn't be published and they always publish it. . . . I don't like foolish propositions. For example, they are asking Anna Magnani to make a picture with Jerry Lewis. . . . I did not like being poor and hungry, but it is still more real, more vivid to me than having money. Compared to pain, money is never very real. I still dream about the war."

Again, we find hidden elements of compatibility, the strong olfactory sense, which each of them seems to own. Mastroianni says that Italian women are absolutely different from other women because they smell different. He claims that their body fragrance is unique. "I believe I'd be able to tell an Italian woman from any other woman even in the dark just by her natural fragrance. It's a sort of homespun odor. I love it."

"It has always worked with us," Sophia said recently. "I don't think any couple has made as many films as we have. It's nice when you know each other so well. You can tell each other things you couldn't tell other partners."

As of this writing, Sophia Loren and Marcello Mastroianni have made nine films together.

A Special Day *1977*

The Remarrying Kind
ELIZABETH TAYLOR and RICHARD BURTON

No TEAM in our time was more glamorous, exciting, newsworthy, sexually titillating, entertaining, peripatetic, comical, or hardworking. Yet as a TEAM, from a strictly professional point of view, they were a failure. With the exception of WHO'S AFRAID OF VIRGINIA WOOLF?—which hardly counts, considering the distinguished origin of the material and the contribution of the brilliant Mike Nichols as director—virtually all the films they made together were undistinguished or failures or both. CLEOPATRA, THE V.I.P.S, THE SANDPIPER, THE TAMING OF THE SHREW, THE COMEDIANS, DOCTOR FAUSTUS, BOOM , HAMMERSMITH IS OUT, and UNDER MILK WOOD.

The difficulty may have been that their off-screen life was so much more colorful and dramatic than anything they were able to provide for the screen that up there they seemed pale by comparison.

Elizabeth Taylor had been a screen player, a juvenile star, and a superstar during the twenty years before she went to work in CLEOPATRA opposite Richard Burton, with earth-shattering, marriage-shattering, life-shattering results.

Richard Burton, surely one of the greatest living actors in the English language, had concentrated mainly on the stage and made films, one gathers, as a matter of economic convenience. He made MY COUSIN RACHEL, THE DESERT RATS, THE ROBE, PRINCE OF PLAYERS, ICE PALACE, THE LONGEST DAY, but his great achievements were taking place in the theatre where he was a constantly surprising, ever-astounding player.

In and about the British theatre community, that white star could be seen shining brightly in the very center of his forehead.

His career began in 1943 in THE DRUID'S REST by Emlyn Williams. Then THE LADY'S NOT FOR BURNING; at Stratford-upon-Avon: HENRY IV, HENRY V, THE TEMPEST. At the Old Vic: HAMLET; OTHELLO, alternating Othello and Iago; FALSTAFF—all signaling the launching of a career in the mold of Kean or Tree or Irving or Olivier.

Elizabeth Taylor, one of the most beautiful women in all the world, is also one of the toughest. Little wonder; she was forged in the crucible of MGM in its dictatorial days. Moreover, she was then no more than a child.

Here is how she remembers the head of the studio, Louis B. Mayer: "I thought he was a beast. He was inhuman. He used power over people to such a degree that he no longer became a man, he became an instrument of power and he had no scruples. He didn't care who he cut down or who he hurt. . . . He never hurt me because maybe, I think, I was too young."

She recalls that she and her mother were astonished to read in the trade papers one morning that she was going to play the lead in a musical film called SALLY IN OUR ALLEY. Young Elizabeth, about fifteen years old, was terrified because she knew she was neither a singer nor a dancer. Her mother attempted to reassure her, telling her that of course the studio would take care of everything, get her ready, have her coached, but Elizabeth, as intelligent as she was beautiful, knew that one does not become a singer or a dancer in five or six weeks of rehearsal. L. B. had once told her she was always to look upon him as a surrogate father, and if she were ever in any trouble or needed anything she was to come to him and he would help her. She reminded her mother of this, and together they made an appointment to see Mayer.

She says his office looked like a bowling alley, with a dais like a throne-plinth at the end of it. She had to walk what seemed like a mile over a white carpet to a huge white oak desk, then look up at the terrifying figure behind it and hear him ask, "What is it?"

"And we said, 'Well, we've read that I was going to do *Sally in Our Alley* and you know if it's true, then I should start to like work on it, doing dancing lessons and singing lessons, or something.' . . . Silence . . . Deadface. And he looked at my mother, and said, 'What do *you* have to say?' and she said, 'Well, we just wondered whether Elizabeth was going to do the film or not and whether we should start any kind of preparation.' And he, all of a sudden, he screamed, 'How *dare* you come into my office and tell me how to run my business!!' Then he pointed at me and said, 'You're *nothing!* I pulled you out of the gutter and you'd've been nowhere if it hadn't been for me.' And I said, 'But, Mr. Mayer, we didn't come up here to ask for anything, just whether I was supposed to do anything and start to work, whatever.' And he yelled, 'Get out of here!' and he started to foam, literally foam, at the mouth. And he said to my mother, "Don't *you* tell *me* how to run my business. You and your daughter are nothing but *guttersnipes!* Get out of here!' And all at once I heard myself say, 'Mr. Mayer, you and your studio can go to *hell!'* and I ran out of the room in tears and cried and cried and cried and cried. Well, then for weeks I was told by every vice-president that I had to go in and apologize to L. B. for telling him and his studio to go to hell, and if I didn't, it would be all over for me. But I never did. In fact, I never saw him or spoke to him again."

An experience of this sort for a fifteen-year-old girl is likely to harden her toward any authority.

Elizabeth Taylor says, "In the old days, when I was growing up there at Metro, the industry was linked to the star system. Hollywood was so isolated then in this superficial and unrealistic pattern, that some studio-groomed players and the biggest stars never saw Europe or even New York except to promote a picture. The star system was a golden studio-protected cocoon."

When Burton was making STAIRCASE outside of London in 1970 for no salary but for a percentage of the film, he said, "I usually play kings or princes or types like that. I've never played a real villain, a heavy, and not only is this fellow a sadist but he's also a homosexual. Interesting type. I'm not sure about this film. We'll see. . . . It seems fairly ridiculous for someone forty-five or fifty to be learning words written by other people, most of which are bad to make a few dollars. I'm not dedicated, I never was. In a sense, I'm totally alienated from the craft that I employ so superficially and successfully. I've got to keep acting, though. The scripts start mounting and I want to take a peek at them. It's compulsive. There *are* a few challenges left, I suppose. I'm forced by ego to play Lear. Macbeth? Yes, I want to do Macbeth. . . .

Acting—it's all so bloody pernicious. Fame is pernicious. So is money. Of course, don't misunderstand—I don't want to be poor. I don't want to repeat *that* performance. Never."

It seems clear from a study of their joint career that Taylor and Burton were ambitious, were trying their damnedest to set and maintain a high standard.

They undertook the celebrated production of THE TAMING OF THE SHREW, working for no up-front money, holding the budget and schedule down to a minimum. They worked well and efficiently under the direction of Franco Zeffirelli, for whom they had broken their vow never to return to Rome after the agonies of CLEOPATRA and the surrounding notoriety and trouble with the paparazzi and the press and the fans and life. But they were anxious to show that they were serious players and meant to create an acting TEAM that would be to the screen what Laurence Olivier and Vivien Leigh had been to the theatre.

The picture came in on schedule and under budget, but for all her many gifts and charms and talents, playing Shakespeare was not one of Elizabeth Taylor's. She had never spoken a line of Shakespeare in public, and looking back on the experience, it seems audacious to think that an actress could undertake a leading Shakespearean role working from scratch.

And consider the remarkable notion of going to Oxford and making a small film of DOCTOR FAUSTUS with themselves as the only professional players and Oxford students as the balance of the cast, shooting on a very low budget in six weeks, working day and night. Elizabeth played the nonspeaking role of Helen of Troy. Commendable, indeed, but was it really the best use of those talents?

When they began to shoot THE TAMING OF THE SHREW, Elizabeth had some special posters printed, which read:

ELIZABETH TAYLOR
in
THE TAMING OF THE SHREW
and introducing Richard Burton

Burton had some posters made up, too. They read:

Now on location in Rome
RICHARD BURTON in
THE TAMING OF THE SHREW
Written by Richard Burton
Edited by Richard Burton
Produced by Richard Burton

and so on—not mentioning her at all.

Elizabeth Taylor then had a third poster printed, which read:

ELIZABETH TAYLOR
Academy Award Winning Actress
and Shakespearean coach to
Richard Burton
in
THE TAMING OF THE SHREW

Actually, this sort of interplay set the mood perfectly for a picture which might have been, but never was.

Elizabeth Taylor: "I'm *not* a 'sex queen' or a 'sex symbol.' I don't think I *want* to be one. I really don't think that's why people come to my movies. Sex symbol kind of suggests bathrooms in hotels or something. I do know I'm a movie star, and I like being a woman, and I think sex is absolutely gorgeous. But as for being a sex goddess, I don't worry myself that way. I don't mean that I'm Marjorie Main. You know girls usually do have bosoms. If you're going to be a sex queen, you do some undressing, some cheesecake—but I've never done any of that stuff. If my husband thinks I'm sexy, that's good enough for me.
"Maybe Richard and I are sex symbols together because we suggest love. At first, illicit love. And it seems curious that our society today finds illicit love more attractive than married love. Our love is married love now, but there is still a suggestion, I suppose, of rampant sex on the wild."

The Taming of the Shrew *1967*

The Taming of the Shrew *1967*

The Taming of the Shrew *1967*

With regard to the production of WHO'S AFRAID OF VIRGINIA WOOLF?, Burton recalls: "When Elizabeth and Ernie Lehman first brought up the possibility of my doing George I said, 'Not on your life. I'm not playing George. I want to write a book—a splendid book—while Elizabeth is doing the film. There's a special sort of fear an actor can have in a part like this. There's a sort of osmosis, a mingling of the play's blood with one's own that does strangely affect one's life for a time. I've seen it happen to me, and I'm the least Method actor that ever was. To wake up in the morning knowing that something dreadful is going to happen that day and gloom around because of it, well, that can be 'Hamlet.' And I genuinely feared the effect George might have on my life with Elizabeth.

"Well, Elizabeth started in on me, and those great eyelashes started to wiggle. Eventually, I thought, well, if I play it in a certain way and am totally unlike Albee's lean and haunted man—if I could play him as a sort of decaying, seedy, gone-to-fat, almost obese intellectual—it might work.

"Elizabeth and I were quite frightened at the beginning. I'm not joking. We thought we'd have to make a pact. A married couple, if they're intelligent, are bound to indulge in some warfare. However much we tried to be logical or pragmatic and say, 'It's just a job,' we both realized that it would be a life, a life lasting for four months at least, an enormous amount of time.

"I really went into it with some sort of dread that something would happen between Elizabeth and myself because of the nature of this piece, but it's an extraordinary thing—I think we're happier now than we've ever been. We've both realized, I think, the difficulty the other has playing these parts. And in the process, became gentler with each other. It's a silly thing, letting a bloody play work on you. This one has exorcised several ghosts, but—I'll knock on wood—the worst is over."

Their marriage was stormy, to say the least, although it is generally reported that they were at their best at work. In private, the Niagara of money and its attendant jewelry and yachts and white Rolls-Royces and villas and whole floors at posh hotels and constant partying and publicity did to them what it would do to any couple who ever lived.

At work, they were disciplined professionals, the admiration always of their supporting casts and crew. When Noel Coward worked with them in BOOM!, he said he found the Burtons a pair of "old pros."

"They know exactly what they're doing every moment, and it's a pleasure to play with them," he said, "not like this Method nonsense."

Yet the pressures proved far too difficult, and after ten years of marriage, they were separated, and soon afterward divorced. But fourteen months later, it was all rekindled and they were remarried. Having gone through the hell of a long separation, they were convinced that this time it was to be permanent.

But then came the complications again and the troubles again, and they were divorced for a second time, apparently for good—yet with two such volatile personalities, who knows for certain?

Even their reconciliation between marriages was more dramatic, more movielike than anything in any film they ever made. No self-respecting screenwriter would set down the details in a scenario and hope to get an audience to stand for it.

It went something like this:

When the divorce became final, they went their separate ways, continuing to work.

Burton recounts that twenty minutes after the divorce, Liz phoned him and asked, "Richard, do you think we did the right thing?" And from that time on, they talked on the telephone at least three times a week. Contact was necessary in view of their complicated business partnership, joint ownership of properties, and adopted children.

During the course of one of the telephone conversations, they tried to analyze the causes of the failure of their marriage and agreed that it was Burton's drinking that was the root cause of it all.

He asked what she thought might happen if he were to give up alcohol completely.

Cleopatra *1962*

Cleopatra *1962*

The V.I.P.s *1963*

The Sandpiper *1965*

Who's Afraid of Virginia Woolf? *1966*

Who's Afraid of Virginia Woolf? *1966*

The Sandpiper *1965*

The Sandpiper *1965*

She suggested that he do it and then they would see.

After many months of drying out, they had another phone conversation, somewhat complex since she was in Leningrad making THE BLUEBIRD and he was in Switzerland.

They met a few weeks later in Switzerland in the house of close friends. After a long session together, they decided to try again. The first person they told was their adopted fourteen-year-old daughter, Maria. "For how long?" asked Maria. Her father answered, "Forever."

The reunion went well for a few days, yet matters were strained, since they were overcautious, overpolite. But on the third day, they launched into one of their classic battles and knew they had become themselves again.

They went off to Israel, where Burton was preparing a movie.

Elizabeth began an interview, saying, "My former husband. No, I mean my *future* husband—oh, I don't know what to call him. I can't say my fiancé, for God's sake. How about, well, my *roommate*?"

Shortly afterward, she and her roommate were remarried.

There are those who believe that actors and actresses should preserve an air of mystery and reveal as little as possible about their private lives. Certainly in the Utopia to come, should this condition be attained, the audience will gain far more pleasure and have more interest in the performance they see on the stage. It is better if they know little about the personal lives of the players.

But in these days of overcommunication, the hunger for inside stuff appears to be insatiable. Everyone wants to know everything about everyone else. There are those who enjoy giving the information, and there are those who are seduced into performing off-stage and off-screen far beyond the need.

The Richard Burton–Elizabeth Taylor story is a classic example of the danger of these poisons. Here were two highly competent, greatly experienced, richly talented players. There is no reason why, given in addition their superior intelligence, they could not have developed into a great film TEAM. Every film director in the world would have been eager to work with them; any film writer would be proud to prepare material for them; any company, glad to have backed them. And there before them was an endless, eager public, anxious to admire, adore, applaud.

Instead, the way of the world led them into off-screen high jinks, ostentation, display, erratic behavior, and truly vulgar activity. It made appreciating them difficult, even for those of us who admired them individually and as a TEAM.

The lost opportunity is what seems most tragic. It is true that he preferred to act on the stage. But there is no reason why she could not have joined him there and become a disciplined stage actress. Alternating with stage work, what would have been wrong with reaching high and making films that producers would not have been willing to make without two great superstars?

One thinks of them in MACBETH, for example, both on the stage and on screen.

People are wont to say, "Well, as the Bible says, money is the root of all evil." But that is *not* what the Bible says. The Bible says, "The *love* of money is the root of all evil." Money *per se,* money by itself, is a valuable commodity. Contrary to popular belief, it *can* buy happiness. It can frequently buy health. It can certainly buy opportunity. The trouble is that once its acquisition begins, it is difficult to know where to stop.

Once, after a late party at Sardi's, my wife and I began walking home and found ourselves threading our way through Shubert Alley. There, to our astonishment, at 2:10 A.M., was Mr. Lee Shubert's car and driver waiting for him. It happened that the following day we lunched with him, and said, "Were you still working at two-ten this morning?"

"Until *three*-ten," he said proudly.

"Why do you do it, Mr. Lee?" asked my wife. "Don't you have enough?"

And Mr. Lee replied, "Ruthie—how much is enough?"

People who cannot answer that question are doomed.

Who's Afraid of Virginia Woolf? *1966*

Who's Afraid of Virginia Woolf? *1966*

Butch Cassidy and the Sundance Kid *1969*

His and His
PAUL NEWMAN and ROBERT REDFORD

Robert Redford, one of the screen's most able and attractive and valuable players, can credit his ascendancy to superstardom to his appearance opposite Paul Newman in BUTCH CASSIDY AND THE SUNDANCE KID.

His film debut took place in 1962 in a low-budget picture—WAR HUNT—made by Terry Sanders and his brother, Denis, and released through United Artists.

Although it had quality and was selected as one of the year's Ten Best Pictures by the National Board of Review, its release was limited.

Before that time, his acting career had been confined to bits and replacements on Broadway, until he made a great personal success in SUNDAY IN NEW YORK by Norman Krasna, in which I directed him and perceived at once a potential film star.

Still the only film opportunity offered him was WAR HUNT.

He returned to the theatre the following year to play BAREFOOT IN THE PARK by Neil Simon, directed by Mike Nichols, and scored again brilliantly.

In the meantime, SUNDAY IN NEW YORK had been made into a film starring Jane Fonda, but Robert Redford was not even considered for it. Even after BAREFOOT IN THE PARK, the best the movie business could come up with for him was a picture in Germany called SITUATION HOPELESS—BUT NOT SERIOUS, something of a catastrophe.

Later that same year, he was offered one of the many parts in INSIDE DAISY CLOVER, starring Natalie Wood. There was some question in his mind whether or not he should play it since the role was that of a homosexual movie star. We discussed it at length. I advised against it, pointing out that if he were an established film star, he could play anything with equanimity. But to begin a career playing a homosexual might easily stamp him as a real one.

He discussed it with the producer and the director, who assured him there was going to be a complete revision of the script and that he would not, in fact, be playing a homosexual. Reassured, he signed for the picture and made it. When it was released, he found to his un-comfortable surprise that the material relating to homosexuality had been restored.

However, I was apparently wrong, because in the end, it did not affect his career.

Following INSIDE DAISY CLOVER, he played in THE CHASE with Marlon Brando, then opposite Natalie Wood in THIS PROPERTY IS CONDEMNED. Finally, when the film of BAREFOOT IN THE PARK was made, he played his original part. The picture succeeded, but he still had not cracked through.

Then came BUTCH CASSIDY AND THE SUNDANCE KID, which had been prepared originally as a project to costar Paul Newman and Steve McQueen. At the last moment, Steve McQueen felt that his part was not as good as Paul Newman's. He offered to switch parts. Newman considered this briefly and declined. McQueen withdrew from the picture, and the search for a replacement was on.

The first idea was Marlon Brando—Brando is aways the first idea—but he was at that time involved with the Black Panthers and their movement in Oakland, California, and could not be contacted. Dick Zanuck, in charge of production at Twentieth Century-Fox, went so far as to send a representative to Oakland to talk to Brando, who said to him, "This picture can be very important for your career, Marlon." To which Brando replied, "America's important, too, and I'm working for America."

More urging, bigger and better offers, but finally it became clear that Marlon Brando was not going to do it.

The studio began to work on trying to get Warren Beatty.

All this time, the director, George Roy Hill, believed that Robert Redford could do it. The studio declined. During conference after conference, Hill stubbornly clung to his Redford idea without success.

At one point, Dick Zanuck said, "Redford's been to the post too many times and never made it. What the hell do you want *him* for? I'll tell you what. I'll pay you off and shelve the picture rather than use him."

Time passed. Hill engaged the support of Paul Newman and, finally, of William Goldman, who had written the original screenplay.

Eventually, it happened.

Lucky for Redford, yes, but luckier still for Twentieth Century-Fox, who were handed on a platter, against their will, the biggest hit they had had in many years.

Following BUTCH CASSIDY AND THE SUNDANCE KID, Redford was in a position to choose his parts and his films, but failed to capitalize on his opportunity. His first picture after BUTCH CASSIDY AND THE SUNDANCE KID was DOWNHILL RACER, a skiing picture, doubtless appealing to him since he himself is an expert skier.

Then came an ambitious film called TELL THEM WILLIE BOY IS HERE, which, for all its merit, failed.

Another failure called LITTLE FAUSS AND BIG HALSY followed, then an obvious attempt at a commercial success called THE HOT ROCK. After that, THE CANDIDATE, a well-meant, serious political statement, but not a success. Now JEREMIAH JOHNSON, into which Redford poured his heart and his faith. It is looked upon now as a kind of *succès d'estime*, but did little to advance his career.

Following this came his curious pairing with Barbra Streisand in THE WAY WE WERE, and at last, a commercial success, although Streisand got most of the credit. It was necessary to wait until he was teamed again with Paul Newman in THE STING to come through with another smashing success, both critical and commercial.

THE GREAT GATSBY, in which Redford was hopelessly miscast, was next. Reunited with George Roy Hill, he made THE GREAT WALDO PEPPER, which did not reach its objective.

But after the enormously daring and audacious and successful ALL THE PRESIDENT'S MEN, Redford's position in films was at last secure.

An examination of the overall output makes it eminently clear that it was his teamings with Paul Newman that propelled him and then repropelled him into a position of great importance.

Robert Redford was born on August 18, 1937, in Santa Monica, California. His father was a milkman, which he claims is the reason he never has liked milk. His mother died at about the time Bob was getting out of high school.

The only show business figure in his family was his grandfather, Charles E. Redford, a violinist who used to play in the pit at Keith's in New London, Connecticut. Bob remembers that he was 5 foot 2 inches tall, had a big nose, and smoked a cigar constantly, always having to take care that it did not get too short; if it did, it burned the tip of his nose. This remarkable little guy lived to be ninety, and the last time Bob called him, he asked, "What are you doing these days, Tiger?" And his grandfather replied, "Haunting houses."

After high school Bob went to the University of Colorado, but since his ambition was painting, he took off for France and Italy and bummed around Europe for a few years. He managed finally to get a show together in Florence and made $200 on it.

He returned to California and took an apartment of his own in Hollywood, continuing to paint. In the same building four girls were sharing an apartment. They had come out to California just for the hell of it. One of them was a beautiful redhead named Lola Van Wagenen from Provo, Utah. The two redheads met. Her recollection of him is something less than enthusiastic: "He had a big red beard, bare feet, and a vest, and he was sure number one on the list of forbidden items my parents gave me when I left Utah."

Whatever her original reservations, when Redford proposed, she accepted, and they were married in September 1958.

Together, they went to New York, where Redford continued his art studies at Pratt Institute, then decided he was not going to make it as a painter and switched suddenly to the American Academy of Dramatic Arts. During this period, Lola got a job in a bank and continued to work there until Redford began to earn a living as an actor.

Meanwhile, they produced two children: Shauna, and then David James; nine years later, Amy Hart.

One of the sights I shall never forget is the one I saw when I walked into Redford's dressing

Butch Cassidy and the Sundance Kid   *1969*

The Sting *1973*

room in Washington while we were trying out SUNDAY IN NEW YORK. There was the redheaded Redford with his redheaded wife and two redheaded adorable children. They looked for all the world like a Norman Rockwell *Saturday Evening Post* cover.

Redford is far more than an actor. He is politically aware and deeply involved in the Citizens Committee to Save Provo Canyon, as well as numerous campaigns designed to protect the environment.

Lola Redford is far more than a movie star's wife. She has a career of her own based on civic projects and is one of the founders of Consumer Action Now (CAN), which publishes a newsletter on the subjects of food, air, water, and the like. In short, two important, valuable citizens.

Although it may be perfectly true that in BUTCH CASSIDY AND THE SUNDANCE KID, he was second in importance to the superstar, Paul Newman, it is equally true that by the time they made THE STING, he had caught up with his chum and shared the partnership on an equal basis from the point of view of talent, invention, imagination, and even box office draw.

Paul Newman's fiftieth birthday in 1975 was a great occasion. For one thing, it had that most desirable of all dramatic events, surprise. No one could believe that this handsome, magnetic, blue-eyed, beautiful hunk of man was fifty years old. His family gave him a merry birthday luncheon in Connecticut and presented him with a wicker wheelchair packed with presents. The same night, his wife, Joanne Woodward, threw a tremendous bash for him in New York. She had Neil Sedaka there to sing a parody on Rodgers and Hart's "The Most Beautiful Girl in the World" called "The Most Beautiful Man in the World," and a couple of choruses of "Them There Eyes."

Paul Newman rose to the occasion, and in the course of his speech, said: "I've had only two experiences during my fifty years. One with Joanne, the other with Redford." He presented Redford with a paperweight featuring a pair of bright blue eyes that opened and winked when placed under a light. On it was inscribed:

"Forget Me Not."

If you happen to look like Paul Newman looks, it is almost inevitable that you are going to become an actor, whether you want to or not. In Newman's case, the "not" comes up quite frequently.

These days, rich and famous and admired, he says, "I look back on my career, and except for a few—very few—roles that I felt were meaningful, I wonder what have I accomplished. I've become famous, something I never wanted, and I've made a lot of money, something I was not opposed to having. But what have I accomplished? An American Celluloid Sex Symbol! Whoopee! . . . I'm not miserable. I'm just not happy. I don't have inner serenity and I don't have the guts to do anything else. What happens is that you get caught in the pull of the power generated by your own success. As an actor, I can pretty much write my own ticket. I can look ahead to what I have left of my life as gravy. It's hard to give up something so sure, something that has been so good to you, to tackle something else you don't know if you have the talent to do. . . . I've been thinking of giving up acting for at least ten years now. At first, I thought I really would, conning myself with the old 'one more picture' bit. . . . The most I can hope for is to have a little fun with it now and then. Some actors, such as Alec Guinness and Laurence Olivier, never seem to exhaust themselves, but I am not of that caliber. If I had my wife's talent, I probably wouldn't feel this way about acting. But I doubt I will ever quit now. I might have had the guts to switch careers if I became interested in auto racing at age thirty instead of forty-five, but I started too late and my enthusiasm exceeds my ability. . . . Politics is another field that interests me. I work diligently for candidates and issues I believe in, but when they asked me to run for the senate of Connecticut a few years ago, I chickened out. I honestly didn't feel I was equipped. It would have been great for me but terrible for the public. If I were young, starting out all over again today, I would become a marine biologist. I've even thought of going back to school and taking it up at this late date. But the truth is I'm too tired to go through what I would have to do to become a marine biologist. The good life has spoiled me."

Speaking of BUTCH CASSIDY AND THE SUNDANCE KID, Paul Newman says: "It didn't matter to me what role I played. If Marlon Brando had been in the picture, I would have played the Sundance Kid. If Warren Beatty had consented to do the picture, I would have played Butch. It didn't make any difference, they were both marvelous parts."

As we know, Redford played the Sundance Kid, helping both of them to their greatest success up to that point. After they had been re-teamed for THE STING, Newman said: "I'd welcome another opportunity to do a picture with Redford, but it would have to be something special, something as good or better than *The Sting*. I wish it would happen because we have such a marvelous time on the set. I'm getting to that age now where it's extremely important to me to have fun while making films. Yes, Redford and I are good friends, but the motion picture business is peculiar—you build very strong relationships for three or four months on a picture, then you don't see the guy for three years."

Curiously, Redford won an Academy Award nomination for THE STING and Newman did not. But Newman, a complete professional, does not take the matter of scrolls or plaques or medals or Oscars seriously.

He was born in Cleveland, Ohio, in 1925, which makes him some twelve years his team-mate's senior. Yet such is the ageless quality of screen stars that they seem roughly the same age always when playing together.

His childhood was undoubtedly complicated by the fact that his father was a German Jew and his mother a Hungarian Catholic. However, she left the Church and for some reason brought him up as a Christian Scientist.

Other than that, his adolescence was standard, but when he went to Kenyon College in Ohio, he majored in both drama and economics. After college came World War II, during which he served for three years as a radio man in naval torpedo planes. Then he went on to the Yale School of Drama to get a master's degree. His principal interest was in directing. He also played with the idea of going back to Kenyon to teach theatre, but the summer before his graduation, he went to New York and got a job in the television show, THE ALDRICH FAMILY, which paid him $50 a week. Live television was burgeoning, and he began to be regularly employed. He never returned to Yale.

He joined the Actors' Studio. "I just got very lucky. For reasons too complicated to go into now, I had only one audition there instead of two. I guess they must have misunderstood sheer terror for honest emotion. When I did my first scene for them later, there must have been some agonizing reappraisal. Once you're in, they can't throw you out. I was bad, really bad. So they have to take the credit or the blame for what I am today. I am the terrier type. I just work away at it doggedly."

In 1953, he was cast in William Inge's play, PICNIC, directed by Joshua Logan, noticed by Warner Brothers, and given a contract. He made his film debut in one of their catastrophic failures, THE SILVER CHALICE, which slowed down his career. Ten years later, when it was going to be shown on television in Los Angeles, Paul Newman tried to use his by-then considerable influence to have it stopped. When he failed, he took trade-paper ads, apologizing for his "lusterless, hopeless performance."

In 1956, having been dropped by Warner's, he played Rocky Graziano in SOMEBODY UP THERE LIKES ME. Oddly enough, Graziano was Marlon Brando's model for his performance of Stanley Kowalski in A STREETCAR NAMED DESIRE, and since Newman was actually playing Graziano, he was almost at once compared to Brando.

Paul Newman is inclined to put down his film career, but in fact, it is distinguished and accomplished. After SOMEBODY UP THERE LIKES ME, he made THE LONG HOT SUMMER, RALLY ROUND THE FLAG BOYS!, THE LEFT-HANDED GUN, CAT ON A HOT TIN ROOF, EXODUS, THE HUSTLER, SWEET BIRD OF YOUTH, in which he repeated his Broadway performance, HUD, HARPER, TORN CURTAIN, COOL HAND LUKE. He directed his wife beautifully in RACHEL, RACHEL. Then BUTCH

CASSIDY AND THE SUNDANCE KID. There are few careers as strong, and it is noteworthy that he never traded, as many film players have done, on his looks alone.

Has any actor ever uttered a more sensible statement than the following? "What the audience sees on the screen isn't really the actor himself. The heroics are the writer's heroics, and the intelligence of the actor may be nothing more than the writer's intelligence."

Compare BUTCH CASSIDY AND THE SUNDANCE KID to THE STING. Both have the same stars and the same director. Both are placed in the nostalgic past. BUTCH CASSIDY in the American West in the late nineteenth century; THE STING in the toddling town of Chicago in the 1930's.

Examined carefully, it can be seen that the plots are somewhat alike. In each case, two con men operate in defiance of the law, more or less successfully. Butch and Sundance are bank robbers; some objection has been raised to the fact they are made so adorable and enviable.

In THE STING, the characters of Hooker, played by Redford, and Gondorff, played by Newman, are true criminals who work fleecing unsuspecting "pigeons."

The principal difference is in the male-female aspect. In CASSIDY, it is Sundance who is the take-charge of the pair, and Butch who is dominated. In THE STING, the roles are reversed; Newman becomes the aggressive force and Redford the passive.

One can envision endless changes being rung on these aspects of relationship. It makes us wish for more.

Max Beerbohm once said that the two most charming words in the English language are: "And *then* . . . ?"

What is it that makes the TEAM of Newman and Redford so effective? The fact that they portray two characters who are equally amoral, equally attractive, and equally humorous? When we observe two people clearly admiring of one another, it leads us to admire both of them, which means admiring the TEAM. When we watch a splendid basketball

The Sting   *1973*

The Sting   *1973*

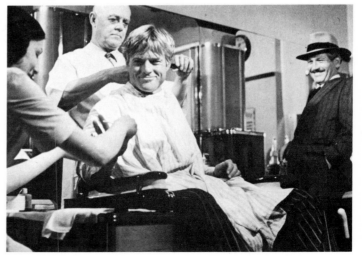
The Sting   *1973*

Butch Cassidy and the Sundance Kid   *1969*

Butch Cassidy and the Sundance Kid   *1969*

Butch Cassidy and the Sundance Kid   *1969*

team in action, what we respond to, even more than the individual prowess, is the teamwork, the interaction, the give and take, the quick understanding, the shorthand communication that exists between people truly close to one another.

Another contemporary man-man TEAM is Jack Lemmon and Walter Matthau. This turns out to be a less interesting TEAM than Newman-Redford simply because Walter Matthau is clearly the dominant figure in the Matthau-Lemmon TEAM, Lemmon apparently willing to take the position of the underdog, the patsy, the schnook, the dominated. Therefore it is less fun to watch, because the balance has been disturbed.

In the Newman-Redford TEAM, each scene has within it the element of limitless possibilities; anything may happen. Redford may get the idea, which Newman may follow. Or Newman may do something audacious, and Redford will not be one bit surprised. In other words, what we see in action is that best of all elements in teaming, complete equality.

We respond to teamwork because we know subliminally and atavistically that no one has ever accomplished anything of worth or value alone, much as many would be glad to have us believe.

Even a painter could not be great if someone else had not manufactured the paint, the brushes, the canvas, and provided the turpentine. Life at its best is teamwork in which members have equal rights, as it were. It is the structure of the democratic form of government under which we live. We are a TEAM, consisting at present of about 200 million members. When we see a superb acting TEAM, such as Newman and Redford, in action, the 200 million become two. They represent TEAM effort, accomplishment, understanding, compassion, humor, a sense of play. When it works, we admire them individually and collectively. When they fail or are frustrated, we bleed for them.

It was probably the outstanding success of Newman-Redford that caused Hollywood actresses of the day to begin to complain vociferously that men had taken over the screen, that there were no parts for women. What was happening? All this was nonsense, and in time, the trend was reversed. Most of the good parts were women's parts and the *men* began to complain that there were no parts for *them*.

A final note to explain the attraction of the Newman-Redford appeal. Without mincing words, it is possible to say that they are playing a special kind of love story. They are in love—which is why we love them.

239

Play It Again, Sam *1972*

The New Breed
WOODY ALLEN and DIANE KEATON

The teaming of Woody Allen and Diane Keaton is the ultimate expression of the style of the seventies. An unconventional leading man opposite a conventional leading lady has a special charm. Had Woody Allen been teamed with, say, Barbra Streisand, the effect would have been diminished. The seventies brought us face to face with the real world more than ever before.

Bernard Shaw's definition of drama—"real things happening to real people"—was largely neglected by American film makers for decades. They believed that the public wanted escape, the perpetration of various myths: love conquers all; love is eternal, every story has a happy ending; murder will out; perpetrators of crime are punished; good girls don't kiss on the first date, good men don't expect them to; young men and women never do it before they get married; and so on ad infinitum.

World War II began to change these ideas, but manners and mores are slow to change, and it took years before figures such as Walter Matthau, Dustin Hoffman, Steve McQueen, Al Pacino, Richard Dreyfuss, and Woody Allen would be considered leading men.

Think of the hope and vision Woody Allen inspires whenever he woos and wins Diane Keaton. It means that you, too, although undersized, underweight, and astigmatic, have a chance at romance. What is glossed over is that it does not hurt to possess Woody Allen's genius, as well. But never mind.

The fact that Woody Allen and Diane Keaton tell us that they were a long on-again-off-again real-life romance is neither here nor there. It is what they do on the screen that is important.

We owe the life and work of this remarkably interesting TEAM to the fact that in cinema, Woody Allen is his own man as producer, writer, director, and actor. He is a major studio all by himself, and if it pleases him to make picture after picture with his partner, Diane Keaton, that is how it goes.

In the so-called "old days," it was the major studios who had dozens of players under contract and were able to form and propagate TEAMS. With the majors virtually gone, it is less simple to accomplish this.

It all began when Woody Allen wrote a play for himself called PLAY IT AGAIN, SAM. It contained a part for a girl and although it was comparatively small, Woody Allen and his director, Joe Hardy, interviewed over fifty actresses. Eventually, Diane Keaton was called back as one of the finalists.

This is how she remembers it: "He had to come up and audition with me, and he was as scared as I was. And I thought he was great—I'd seen him on television before and I thought he was really cute, you know. He looked good to me. I liked him. Mainly he was as scared as me, which I found real appealing."

Woody Allen's version: "I was scared because—first of all, I'd never acted in my life. I was strictly a nightclub comic. And then when we called her back, we were worried that she'd be too tall, you know, and we didn't want the joke of the play to be that I was in love with a, you know, super-looking woman. And so we got on stage together, and *both* of us were nervous—I felt, oh, this is a real actress, she was in *Hair* and I'm just going to waste her time. . . . And we measured back to back, and it was like being in the third grade. And we were just about the same height, so that was it."

Diane admits freely that she had an immediate crush on Woody, and Woody made no secret of his affection for her.

"She'd come in every day," he remembers, "with an absolutely spectacularly imaginative combination of clothes. They were just great—she was the type who'd come in with, you know, a football jersey and a skirt and combat boots, and you know, oven mittens. . . . And I thought she was very charming to be around, and of course, you always get the impulse with Diane to protect her. And she was so bright and so quick. She's also a real easy laugher, which is very seductive. And we kind of drifted together is what happened."

They acted in PLAY IT AGAIN, SAM for a year.

It was during this time that Woody's second marriage—to Louise Lasser—was coming apart, a painful experience for both since they had respect and admiration for each other,

Play It Again, Sam   *1972*

Love and Death   *1975*

personally and professionally.

She had been his partner in his movie BANANAS, and it may be supposed they had dreams of becoming a TEAM, but the so-called chemistry was missing.

After PLAY IT AGAIN, SAM, Diane landed a small part in the film LOVERS AND OTHER STRANGERS, following which she made the film version of PLAY IT AGAIN, SAM with Woody. In the movie, he built up her part considerably.

They next did SLEEPER together, and after that, LOVE AND DEATH.

She appeared in THE GODFATHER, but the impression still seemed to be that she was making it as Woody Allen's protégée, a euphemism for girlfriend.

"I don't believe that at all," Diane said. "I feel that everybody has a career based on somebody, and we're influenced by somebody, and I have to feel that I have the talent to back it up. And I feel I've worked hard. I don't agree with that. Otherwise, I'd kill myself."

Allen agreed: "I have not been a crutch for her at all. It's been absolutely above-board. You could reverse that and think that she's been a crutch to me in many ways. I mean, she's been an enormously supportive person to *me* on projects."

Diane Keaton's real name is Diane Hall, which is why ANNIE HALL is called ANNIE HALL. She grew up in Santa Ana, California. Keaton is her mother's maiden name. Her people were well off; her father, Jack Hall, the head of a civil engineering firm; her mother, Dorothy, a successful photographer. She went to high school in Santa Ana; then for a year and a half to a junior college. But she wanted to be an actress, and at nineteen came east to study at the Neighborhood Playhouse.

Her first job was in the summer theatre at Woodstock, New York. That fall, Broadway proved to be a closed door. She returned to California. Finally, her parents said they would stake her to another chance in New York. She returned, and four months later got her first professional job and made a Broadway debut in HAIR.

She often seemed faintly familiar to au-

diences, and the more perceptive members recognized her as the housewife wearing a track suit in the "Hour After Hour" deodorant commercial. She reminisces: "You know what I got my most money for? That commercial. Twenty-five thousand dollars. I didn't want to do it and I told them so. They said, 'We're going to make it worth your while,' and I did it. I succumbed. But I don't want to do any more commercials, no matter how much the money is."

While she was at the Neighborhood Playhouse, two brothers, Guy and Pip Gillette, formed a rock band called "The Road Runners," and Diane joined up with them. "There were four, plus me. I was a feature sort of thing they'd bring out once in a while. I played tambourine and danced. I sang a couple of Aretha Franklin songs and 'In the Midnight Hour.' Let me tell you, that was real bad. I was not, needless to say, a very good rock 'n' roll singer. But I loved it. We'd play around, but not in the city. We'd get ten dollars a gig."

This experience got her the job in HAIR.

The discussion surrounding the extraordinary ANNIE HALL is just how autobiographical it is. Woody kept the title of the film a secret while it was being made; in fact, the filming was generally done under wraps.

Woody Allen: "People tell me all the time that *Annie Hall* is autobiographical, and I keep telling them that it's not really very autobiographical, but nobody wants to hear that. And one review, one out-of-town review that I'd gotten, said that in order to really enjoy the picture you had to know a lot about Diane's and my private life together—and of course this is completely untrue because I would say eighty percent of the film is totally fabricated."

On the other hand, Jack Hall, Diane's father, says: "It's eighty-five percent true—even to Dorothy and my mother."

We shall never know, and in fact, does it matter? What does matter is that working together, they created one of the most original and important works of art of the decade.

Diane: "None of the facts in *Annie Hall* are true, but the essence of the characters and the relationship is pretty similar. Their feel-

ing, I mean, about each other. There was no problem with me acting inarticulate, you know, and sort of self-conscious and embarrassed and laughing a lot, and so forth. The hard part was letting myself do it without getting in my own way, you know, and ending up doing it off the top. I didn't want to stop myself from going all the way with it. I didn't want to put any stops on my reactions. I just wanted to do it as fully as I could. First, it affects couples so much because everybody knows, I think, how difficult it is to have a relationship and to keep it alive and continuing. So there's a universal fact of life that says breaking up happens to everybody, so no one should feel like a failure when it does happen.

"Then, it's also sort of *Pygmalion,* you know. He teaches her and guides her, but then she goes off on her own and finds the relationship becoming too insular, too confining, too negative, and so she proceeds out into her own life. But in the end, they're still friends, they still like each other, and they know they can't go back to the way it once was. That's touchy, you know. It's sort of bittersweet. The idea that you still have a lot of affection for this person, and you both know that too much time and change has taken place. But life is time and change and it just cannot always be worked out, no matter how much affection there may be. I personally feel that I want to have my own life and work and be with somebody who thinks of me as an equal, you know. And that's what's important for everybody."

Woody Allen was born in New York City in 1935. His name is Allen Stuart Konigsberg. At an early age, he began writing and making contributions to comedy television shows. He began in films with WHAT'S NEW, PUSSYCAT? for which he worked on the story and screenplay, as well as playing in it. He then made an appearance in CASINO ROYALE, following this with a curious job of camping a Japanese spy film by dubbing it and making cut-in appearances. It was called WHAT'S UP, TIGER LILY? He then went out on his own with TAKE THE MONEY AND RUN, and followed it with BANANAS.

From then on, he has continued to con-

tribute to the screen almost annually, and has become one of the most original film artists of the past two decades.

About himself, he says: "I was very shy at ten, a terrible student, a problem in school. At twenty, I was finally thrown out of school. From twenty to thirty, I was a television writer, making the painful transition to being a comedian. At thirty, I had just completed *What's New, Pussycat?* and vowed I would never work in movies unless I could be the director and control the picture. Since then, I've directed all my own films."

Apparently, the backgrounds of the teammates are not unalike. Diane was also shy in youth and would put on little theatrical productions at the age of five, but only in the living room, singing and dancing, imitating the television children's shows she was then watching. At the age of six she took part in a recital at Sunday school, but went up in her lines: "I just burst into tears and broke down sobbing, and they had to take me off the stage."

Still, there was no question as she grew older that acting was what she was destined to do. She joined the Little Theater Guild and a choir called the Debutantes. In the Debutantes, all the girls had to look alike, but Diane refused. If the others were going to wear beige stockings, she would wear black; if their hair was worn down, she put hers up. And her eye makeup was always odd. She was straining for a persona even then.

Allen and Keaton prove the theory that for a TEAM to survive and prosper, it is necessary for them to go off from time to time and prove themselves individually, strengthen their personae. Woody Allen in THE FRONT, and Diane Keaton spectacularly in LOOKING FOR MR. GOODBAR, and surprisingly, in a nightclub appearance, singing at the popular Reno Sweeney in New York.

Both Diane Keaton and Woody Allen are considered Hollywood outsiders, and ANNIE HALL anti-Hollywood.

In a business based upon self-ingratiation, it is refreshing to find someone with the courage to speak his convictions. He makes no

Sleeper   *1973*

Sleeper   *1973*

secret whatever in interviews or in discussions of his dislike for Hollywood.

"I have to admit," he says, "that I really do still feel resentful about so many of my friends moving to Los Angeles. They've been seduced by television, a life more pleasant than in New York City. And I, as you know, don't feel an aim in life is to be happy or to have nice weather, or that kind of stuff. So I have a mild antipathy. If not New York, I would live in Paris. I would not want to live in a culture where I have to drive a car all the time to get places and there was a kind of relentless weather that was the same all the time, or where I couldn't jaywalk without thinking I'm going to have to explain it to somebody."

In 1978, ANNIE HALL was up for Oscars in many categories; for best picture; best screenplay; best actress: Diane Keaton; best actor: Woody Allen; best director: Woody Allen.

Some weeks before the event, in fact even before the voting was completed, Allen made it clear that he was not planning to attend the ceremonies. His producers and backers were horrified, not so much because he had decided not to go, but because he announced it so blatantly, doubtless offending a good many Academy members, who although they might have voted for him and his picture in one or more categories, surely would *not* vote for anyone so cavalier and ungracious. Woody explained that on that night, which happened to be a Monday, he normally played clarinet with a group at Michael's Pub and saw no reason to change his routine. Further, he was working on a new picture and would prefer not to interfere with that. This was thought to be extremely disrespectful, even rude.

Yet such is the power of excellence that ANNIE HALL won for Best Picture; Woody Allen won as Best Director, as co-writer of the screenplay; and Diane Keaton as Best Actress.

Woody says, "I've always thought she was born to be a movie star. She's got a real *American* quality."

Is there a wisp of a clue to their basic incompatibility in this statement by Diane? "I have this feeling—I don't know if I really want to stay in New York. My little dream has always been to have a house on the ocean in California —not a big one, just a little house with about three or four dogs. And a little old car. That's my dream. I don't know what's stopping me. I could do that now. Maybe when I get a little more straightened out . . ."

Yin and Yang. Yes and no. Male and female. Affirmative and negative. Up and down. In and out. Backward and forward. Inhale, exhale. These are the opposites, and unless each member of a TEAM represents one, and the other the other, it fails.

It is interesting to consider this TEAM's development from PLAY IT AGAIN, SAM to ANNIE HALL. The comparison is dramatic, for although PLAY IT AGAIN, SAM is amusing, interesting, and competent, it is a will-o'-the-wisp compared to the solidly crafted, tremendously affecting film, ANNIE HALL. Both players have been enriched by their contact with one another. It is not so much a question of conscious influence or unconscious imitation, but has to do with the constantly flowing, life-giving, empathic exchange of energy that takes place when two players are brilliantly matched.

It took Tracy and Hepburn seven films to achieve the height they reached, and had they made seventy more, the height would have been still higher.

Alfred Lunt and Lynn Fontanne spent a lifetime acting together, and their last efforts were their best.

These are all matters of metaphysics and of magic, and it is fair to say that no one, not even Woody Allen or Diane Keaton themselves, will ever know how much they owe to one another.

Annie Hall *1977*

Annie Hall *1977*

TOMORROW'S TEAMS?

INDEX

255